Heirloom Machine Quilting

*A Comprehensive Guide to Hand-Quilted Effects
Using Your Sewing Machine*

by
Harriet Hargrave

C&T PUBLISHING

We have made every attempt to properly credit the trademarks and brand names of the items listed in this book. We apologize to any that have been listed incorrectly and would appreciate hearing from you.

Bernina is a registered trademark of Fritz Gegauf, Ltd. DMC is a registered trademark of the DMC Corporation. Sulky is a registered trademark of Sulky of America. Madeira is a registered trademark of Madeira Threads (U.K.) Ltd. Kanagawa is a brand name of YLI Corporation. Natesh is a registered trademark of Kaleidoscope. DBK is a trademark of Inglis Publications Products. Exacto is a registered trademark of Hunt Manufacturing. Mylar is a registered trademark of E.I. duPont de Nemours & Co. Sharpie is a registered trademark of Sanford Corporation. Mark-B-Gone is a trademark of Dritz Corporation. Tear-Away is a brand name of Sew Art International. Supracolor is a registered trademark of Caran D'Ache. Washout Cloth Markers is a brand name of Dixon/Ticonderoga. Charcoal White is a registered trademark of the General Pencil Co. Carb-Othello is a registered trademark of Schwan-Stabilo. Multi-Pastel Chalks is a registered trademark of the General Pencil Co. Karismacolor is a registered trademark of Berol USA, Division of Berol Corporation. Fade-Away is a trademark of White Sewing Products Co., a division of White Sewing Machine Co. Orvus WA Paste is a registered trademark of Proctor & Gamble. Mountain Mist is a registered trademark of Sterns Technical Textile Co. Cotton Classic is a registered trademark of Fairfield Processing Corporation. Taos Mountain Traditional and Designer Light are registered trademarks of Taos Mountain Wool Works. Glazene process is a registered trademark of Sterns Technical Textile Co. Quilt-Light is a registered trademark of Sterns Technical Textile Co. Extra Loft, Low Loft and Hi Loft are registered trademarks of Fairfield Processing Corporation. Poly-Down is a registered trademark of Hobbs Bonded Fibers. Traditional is a trademark of Fairfield Processing. Pellon is a registered trademark of Freudenberg Nonwovens, Pellon Division. Thermore is a registered trademark of Hobbs Bonded Fibers. Loftguard is a registered trademark of Hoechst/Celanese. OUIJA is a registered trademark of Parker Brothers Division of Kenner Parker Toys Inc. Easy Wash is a registered trademark of Airwick Industries, Inc. Ensure is a registered trademark of Sterns Technical Textiles Co. Snowy Bleach is a registered trademark of Airwick Industries,Inc. Velcro is a registered trademark of Velcro USA Inc.

Published by C & T Publishing
P.O. Box 1456
Lafayette, CA 94549

Library of Congress Catalog Card Number: 90-62172

Front Cover Photo: Brian Birlauf
BLUE MEDALLION
68" x 84"
by Harriet Hargrave

Photograpy: Brian Birlauf, Birlauf and Steen, Denver, Colorado unless otherwise credited

Back Cover Photo: Rizzo Photography, Riverside, CA, courtesy of Bradley Printing, Des Plains, Il

Editing: Nadene M. Hartley

Copyediting: Jane Palmer Parkinson

Cover/Text Design: Jim Love/Publishers Design Studio

Illustration: Randy Miyake/Miyake Illustrations

Composition and Electronic Page Make-up: Publishers Design Studio, Mill Valley, California

Printed in The United States

ISBN 0-914881-33-7

10 9 8 7 6 5 4 3 2 1

Contents

Color section starts on page 43

 HIS BOOK IS DEDICATED to my mother, Frances Frazier. Without her constant support, love, and dedication to her family, I would not have the love for quilts that I share with her, nor the luxury of pursuing a career in the areas that I love: teaching, traveling, and quilting.

Introduction

THE RESPONSE I RECEIVED from the first writing of *Heirloom Machine Quilting* exceeded my wildest dreams. Previously, I had spent a great deal of time trying to be low profile and not make waves in the hand quilting world. In 1986, machine quilting was appearing here and there, but very seldom did quality machine-quilted quilts appear at local and regional shows, let alone at national shows. When I started traveling and teaching nationally in 1985, I introduced the art of machine quilting to anyone who was curious as to how I got my quilts to look hand quilted. In fact they were quilted in a matter of hours using my best friend, my Bernina® sewing machine. I still remember feeling I had to defend and sell the concept in most areas.

Four years later, the national exposure to machine quilting had increased to the point that Caryl Bryer Fallert won the Best of Show at the 1989 American Quilter's Society quilt show in Paducah, Kentucky, with her quilt, Corona II: The Solar Eclipse. This coveted award, when given to a machine-quilted quilt, caused quite a reaction — both positive and negative — in the quilt world. Instead of seeing what a magnificent piece it was regardless of technique, many quilters had trouble accepting the fact that it was machine-quilted. I look forward to the day when all quilters, hand and machine, look at what the actual quilting lends to the quilt. The quality of the work and the skill that it takes to achieve the final product should be appreciated. I feel that we spend too much energy debating whether machine or hand is best. There are enough quilts in all our heads that need to come out, that as long as the workmanship is of high quality, it should not matter what technique was used.

The first edition of *Heirloom Machine Quilting* contained the general directions to achieve quality machine quilting. I was honored when Caryl Fallert mentioned it in her interview with AQS after winning. She said, "I believe a real breakthrough for quilters came when Harriet Hargrave's book was published with complete and concise directions for machine quilting." Her statement affirmed that I had done what I was hoping to do in that book.

However, after four years on the road teaching, and after hundreds of students have asked thousands of questions, I found that more complete information and guidance was needed. And realizing that I can't be everywhere, and that teachers needed more support, I am delighted to have the opportunity to rewrite the book. I hope to answer the many questions that have come to me from quilters trying to master these techniques.

I wish you the best of luck in your pursuit of mastering machine quilting. It will provide you with limitless hours of enjoyment and satisfaction and will let you get many more quilts out of your head and onto your beds and walls, where they can be enjoyed by all.

PART ONE

Getting Ready

Work Space and Equipment

YOU ARE NOT MACHINE QUILTING, *you are hand quilting with an electric needle.* If you think about it this way, you will understand why your work space is so important. The space and equipment used for machine quilting is as important to your success as that used for hand quilting. Maybe more so, since machine quilting creates much more bulk and many maneuvering problems. Your work space should be a well-lighted room that can accommodate a large quilt.

The way in which your machine is set up will make a real difference in the ease of quilting. If you are serious about doing a lot of machine quilting, obtain a cabinet for your machine. When your machine is set up in a portable situation, you do not have enough support for the bulk of the quilt. Nor do you have room for your hands to glide the fabric where it is needed during the quilting. If the machine is lowered into a cabinet, the table surface is level with the throat plate of the machine. The quilt will be supported by the table and leave your hands free to quilt. Your hands will not slip off the edge of the machine while moving the quilt around under the needle.

Extend this working surface by placing additional tables around the cabinet. Place one behind the machine, and one to the left of the cabinet, so that the quilt cannot fall onto the floor and drag against the needle while quilting.

If a cabinet is not possible, you can purchase an extension, such as the one in Figure 1.2. This exten-

sion is produced by Uni-Unique Products, and uses a Parsons insert that will allow it to fit any machine. The insert can be ordered from your local sewing machine dealer to fit almost any model of machine.

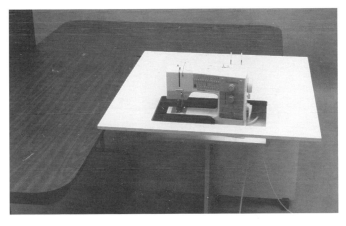

FIG. 1.1 Level sewing surface

FIG. 1.2 Uni-Unique extension table

You can create your own extension by going to the lumber yard and purchasing a sheet of masonite. This product is slick on the surface, allowing the fabric to glide easily. You will need a piece that extends out from the front of the machine about 4 inches, to the left 18 to 24 inches, and behind the machine 12 to 18 inches. Make a template of the arm of your machine and transfer it onto the masonite. Cut an opening in the masonite so that it will fit up tight around the arm of your machine. Cut dowels to the proper height and screw onto the masonite for legs. This gives you an excellent working surface that will support your quilt and enable you to move your hands freely as you quilt.

Equally important is your chair. Machine quilting strains your back and upper arms if you do not sit properly. Purchase a high quality secretarial chair. It should have five legs, instead of four, to prevent tipping. Check that the size of the seat fits your body. If the seat is too small, it will cut off circulation to your legs. A pneumatic lift allows you to position the height of the chair to the most comfortable level with just the lift of a lever. The back of the chair should be able to go up and down, as well as forward. This adjustment is needed to eliminate back strain while quilting.

This may all seem like a lot of bother, but reaching up with your arms to place and move the quilt under the machine needle puts a lot of stress on your back and between your shoulder blades. Also, you have much better vision and control when you look down on your work. Lift your chair high enough so that you can see down on the presser foot and fabric. Make sure that glare from the light

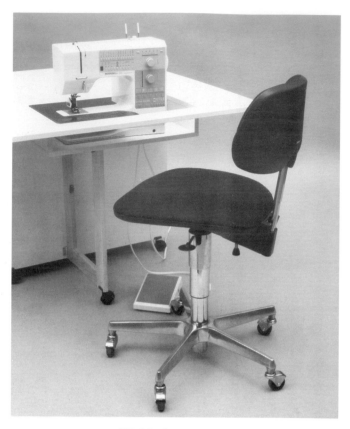

FIG. 1.3   Secretarial chair

bulb on the machine does not cause vision problems, and sit directly in front of the needle, not centered in front of the machine.

Finally, place your machine far enough back so that you can lean forward. Rest your elbows or forearms on the edge of the table, and rest your upper body weight on them. Relax your arms and hands. Place your hands on the quilt as though you are playing a piano. The finger tips should be on the surface, wrists up with the fingers ready to walk wherever you need them.

Your Sewing Machine

THE QUALITY OF YOUR EQUIPMENT makes a big difference in its performance. A machine that has constant tension problems, gets hot after sewing for long periods of time, doesn't have the necessary attachments, won't sew well using different threads on top and bottom, etc., is not going to give you a rewarding experience. Just as woodworkers do not work with discount quality tools, machine quilters should not expect to do beautiful work with a lesser quality machine.

Suggested machine features:

1) Perfect tension adjustment, no matter what combinations of threads are put into the machine.
2) Automatic needle stop, so that when you stop sewing, the needle stops instantly and does not coast on for two more stitches.

3) Up and down needle position on command. (My machine allows me to do this with the foot control. One tap puts the needle down into the fabric, another tap brings it up to the highest position without my ever removing my hands from the fabric. This helps control the quilt.)

4) The ability to sew for hours at high speed without overheating.

5) High quality accessories that are made strictly for your brand.

6) A reputable dealer who will help with minor adjustments, and understand what you are doing.

I do not advise using Singer Featherweights for machine quilting. The feed dog system is straight, and walking feet do not fit properly on this machine. Walking feet needed for machine quilting are designed for a zigzag system, and are too wide for the narrow dogs on the Featherweight. The feed dogs do not drop, making work with a darning foot more difficult. There is very little space available inside the arm of the machine for any bulk to fit. Finally, the motor is small. You can cause excess wear and tear on a machine that is not built to run at high speeds for long periods of time. Keep your Featherweights for piecing and general sewing.

Before starting the exercises in the next chapters, prepare your machine. First, clean it thoroughly inside and out. Refer to your manual or ask your dealer where you should clean and oil. The lint from your machine should be cleaned after each bobbin is emptied or it will pull the oil from the metal and cause excess wearing. Keep the machine well oiled, but not over-oiled.

Even the "non-oiling" machines need extra oil when put through this process. They should be taken to the dealer at the first sign of any trouble, such as a foreign noise. Machine quilting can be hard on a machine, so extra care is warranted. Again, contact your dealer and have him show you the best way to care for your equipment when it is used for this purpose.

Tension is a mystery to many sewers. I feel that dealers have done us a disservice by not teaching us to adjust tension properly. You should know what the dials are, and how to use them. The numbers are there for reference when adjusting. Experiment with your machine for a few minutes to get comfortable with their function.

Sew a row of stitches in two layers of fabric. Correct tension is evident when both threads are linked together in the center of the layered fabrics. Too much top thread tension will cause the top thread to run on the surface of the fabric, while the bottom thread is pulled up to a loop over it. (This can also be caused by loose bobbin tension.) Too much bottom tension will cause the bottom thread to run on the underside of the fabric while the top thread is pulled down to loop under it. If the top tension is too loose, this can also occur.

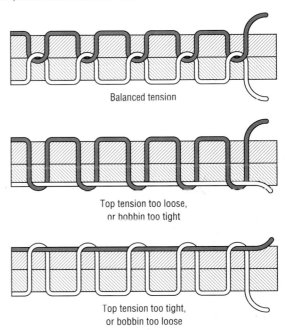

Balanced tension

Top tension too loose, or bobbin too tight

Top tension too tight, or bobbin too loose

FIG. 1.4 Effects of bobbin tension

You can check your own bobbin tension and correct it if necessary. With the high speed and long duration of sewing times, bobbin tension can work itself out of adjustment. Knowing how to check and adjust it can save a lot of time and grief.

Thread a full bobbin into the bobbin case. Make sure it is threaded properly. When inserting the bobbin into the bobbin case, the bobbin should turn clockwise as you are looking at it. This allows the thread to come off the bobbin then go back on itself as it enters the slit and goes under the tension clip. (See Figure 1.6).

Let the bobbin case hang down freely by the thread. It must not slide down by its own weight, but when you jerk your hand lightly upward, yo-yo style, it should gently fall. If it doesn't move at all, the tension is too tight. If it falls easily, it is too loose. (See Figure 1.5).

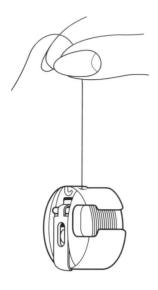

FIG. 1.5 Finding correct bobbin tension

The large screw on the tension clip adjusts the tension. Turn it to the right to tighten and to the left to loosen. Adjust in very small increments until the tension is correct. Once the bobbin tension is correct, any adjustments that need to be made can be done on the top only. Make it a habit to check machine top and bobbin tensions before beginning each project.

Unbalanced tension can be used for decorative effect when using different threads. For example, use clear thread on top and black cotton thread in the bobbin. If the top tension is tightened and a large needle is used, the black thread is pulled to the top in tiny loops, creating the look of a tiny, hand-running stitch.

Don't be afraid to experiment and play with your machine. It is a wonderful tool that has the potential to create anything you can imagine. Take classes and sit in on demonstrations from various dealers. They all have tricks you can apply to your machine.

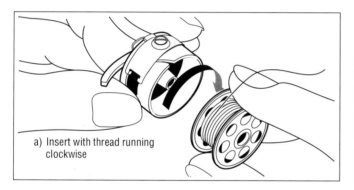

a) Insert with thread running clockwise

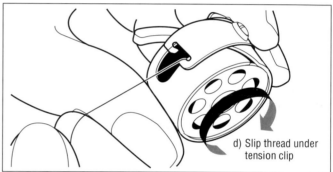

d) Slip thread under tension clip

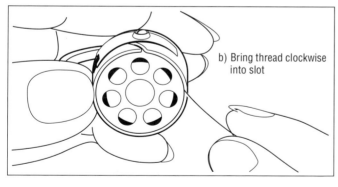

b) Bring thread clockwise into slot

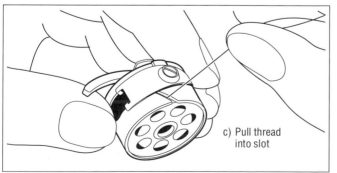

c) Pull thread into slot

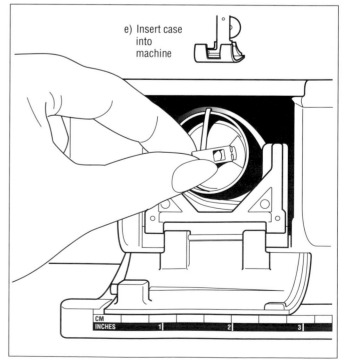

e) Insert case into machine

FIG. 1.6 Correct threading of bobbin

Accessories

SEVERAL ACCESSORIES AVAILABLE for sewing machines are especially helpful for machine quilting. If you do not find these accessories in your attachment box, check their availability with your local sewing machine dealer.

WALKING FOOT

The walking or even feed foot is an attachment which allows all three layers of a quilt to move evenly under the foot without shifting and pushing. This foot is a must if you plan to do a lot of machine quilting with the use of the feed dogs as in straight-line grid and ditch quilting. The walking foot is used for any straight-line quilting.

This foot fits onto the machine much like a ruffler. There are two "feet" on the attachment. One foot is down when the needle is down and a stitch is being made. The other foot is down when the needle is

up and the feed dogs are taking a step. This is controlled by a lever that is connected to the needle clamp screw on your machine. As the lever goes up and down, so does the mechanism of the foot.

A walking foot reproduces the motion of the feed dogs on top of the fabric. It keeps the top and bottom layers even. The biggest problem in machine quilting is the pushing of the top layer by the pressure of the presser foot while the feed dogs are gathering up the lining. While the machine is forming a stitch, the feed dog is down and the foot holds the fabric against the throat plate. As the needle comes up, so do the feed dogs. The walking foot then lifts the main foot and sets down another set of feet that line up with the feed dogs. The top fabric is now being fed evenly with the bottom fabric, while allowing the main foot to lift and walk over any slight fullness without sewing in a tuck or pushing the fabric out of place.

Many sewing machine companies have walking feet available for their machines. For optimal performance, buy the brand that is made for your machine. If your brand does not manufacture the foot for your machine, you will need to get a "generic" foot that fits standard low and high shank machines. When installing a walking foot, mount it on your machine and lower the presser bar. Make sure that the inside feeders align exactly with the feed dogs. Otherwise, the pressure does not distribute evenly, and the foot cannot work properly. A poorly fitting walking foot can be worse than no foot at all.

FIG. 2.1 Variety of walking feet

DARNING FOOT

When using a regular presser foot, it is next to impossible to turn a quilt under the machine to do intricate, fancy quilting designs. This requires free fabric movement under the foot. A darning foot creates the magic of free-motion quilting, and is necessary when attempting to stitch three layers together.

To form a proper stitch, the fabric must be flat against the throat plate as the needle passes through the throat plate hole. The clearances for a properly formed stitch are critical. If the fabric is allowed to lift as the needle comes up, a stitch is skipped. The darning foot rises with the needle, allowing free motion of the work, then lowers with the needle to hold the fabric down on either side of the needle as it enters the fabric. Drop the feed dogs when using this foot.

If you cannot locate a darning foot for your machine, try using a clear plastic foot, like an open-toe appliqué foot, and remove all the pressure off the foot by releasing the spring on the top of your machine. Check your manual. A darning spring is also available as a last resort. It is not as effective at compressing the batting while stitching, but it does add finger protection and improves the stitch quality.

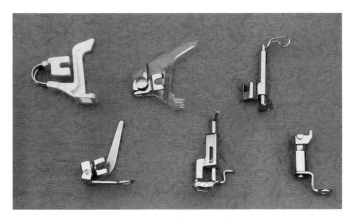

FIG. 2.2 Variety of darning feet

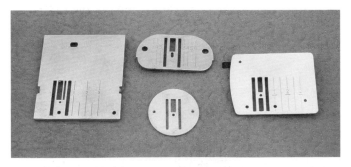

FIG. 2.3 Straight stitch throat plates

Some manuals say to darn without a foot at all. Beware of this. You will notice that when they illustrate this, the fabric is in a hoop. When quilting with a bare needle, you lose maneuverability from the lack of support that the darning foot provides, and your fingers are susceptible to being hit with the needle.

THROAT PLATES

The use of a straight stitch throat (needle) plate helps eliminate puckers and tension problems. The straight stitch throat plate has a tiny round hole to accommodate the needle when straight stitching. (A zigzag throat plate has an oval hole to accommodate the needle swing when zigzag stitching.) Because there is room for only the needle to pass through, a neater and faster stitch is made, enabling the thread to lock tightly.

When sewing straight lines or quilting with a zigzag plate, the fabric is allowed to push down with the needle into the oval opening. This hinders the needle's ability to make a clean, locked stitch, and the tension can be thrown off when this happens. The bobbin thread tends to lie on the underside and can have the appearance of being "couched" by loops of the top thread, especially when using free-motion quilting techniques with a darning foot.

The straight stitch throat plate gives you a higher quality stitching line when piecing your quilts. When piecing template shapes, it is also very helpful in preventing the first ¼ inch of a point from being "eaten" when the needle pierces the point.

NEEDLES

Use only high quality machine needles and start each project with a new needle. Use the needle type, size and brand recommended for your machine to prevent poor quality and/or skipped stitches.

Size 80/12 needles are recommended for machine quilting. Do not use needles larger than 80/12s. If you find that needle holes appear in certain fabrics, you may want to change to a 70/10. A finer needle is more fragile, so care must be taken when using it. If you are a beginner, I do not advise using 70s yet.

When quilting for a long period of time using polyester threads and battings, you might find the thread breaking or even melting.

This can be caused by the high heat buildup from the friction of high-speed sewing through synthetic fibers. If this happens to you, try using a 75/11 blue steel Schmetz needle. It retains a cooler surface when sewing through synthetics. A needle lubricant applied to the needle might also solve your problems.

THREADS

Quilters often give little thought to the purchase of thread, but it is very important to the longevity of a quilt. You should buy the highest quality thread available for all your sewing projects, but be especially careful when purchasing thread for your quilts.

Choose a thread that is less strong than the fabric of your quilt top, preferably 100% mercerized cotton. I use this thread for both piecing and quilting. Years from now, after much use and many launderings of the quilt, you will appreciate your choice of thread. It is possible to repair a quilting line where the thread has broken, but it is impossible to repair the fabric that has been "cut'" by a thread that was stronger than the fabric. Think of garments that you may have had that when extra stress was put on a seam, the fabric ripped. Chances are the thread was too strong and abrasive, and it wore down the fibers of the fabric.

Size 50, 3-ply cotton mercerized thread is recommended for all light-to-medium-weight cotton fabrics. Cotton thread is strong, smooth, lustrous and resists shrinkage. Never buy bargain thread for machine sewing. It is usually made from short fibers which make it weak and abrasive. Check the thread for long, staple fibers; it should not have a fuzzy appearance. If it is smooth, with very few fibers appearing, it is generally a high-quality thread. This applies to both cotton and polyester threads.

Use cotton-wrapped polyester thread only when using polyester blends in the quilt top and lining. It is too thick for cotton fabrics, and can cause puckered seams and abrasion.

Two guidelines to help you in choosing threads are:

1) Choose thread that is the same fiber type as the fabric you are sewing.
2) Thread should be weaker than the fabric.

INVISIBLE NYLON

Invisible nylon is the only exception I make to the use of cotton threads in cotton quilts. But be very careful and critical of the quality you purchase. Use only the finest, highest quality nylon available. It is made strictly for artwork, not for sewing draperies and hems.

There is a vast difference in weights and qualities of nylon thread. The size needed is .004. When buying, try to break the thread. It should break very easily. It should not be at all course or stiff. Avoid buying nylon thread that comes on large cones, as the weight is slightly different from the small tubes, and the thread can become brittle after it is stored on the cone for long periods. Always try to buy and use fresh thread in smaller amounts. Look for thread packaged on 3-inch long cardboard tubes, wrapped with cellophane (see Figure 2.4). It should not be on a regular thread spool, and it should not jump off the spool like a spring when the package is opened. Your local quilt shop or machine arts store and many sewing machine dealers carry this product.

The nylon thread needs to be weaker than the bobbin thread. Regular nylon sewing thread is like fishing line and is very difficult to break. It also feels tough and coarse. If you use this thread and stress is applied to the quilt, the thread will tear the fabric and pop the bobbin thread. The soft invisible nylon

FIG. 2.4 Threads, needles, thread clips

thread, however, stretches with stress and works with the bobbin thread.

Invisible nylon is the only thread that gives machine quilting a hand-quilted appearance. Invisible nylon is a continuous nylon filament that comes in clear or smoke color. The clear thread is used on light-colored fabric; the smoke thread is used on darker fabrics. All that can be seen is the depression of the quilting line, not the thread itself. The thread takes on the color of each fabric it is sewn into. A regular cotton thread would be highly visible when crossing many colors of fabric, and would detract from the beauty of the quilt.

Although invisible nylon thread can be used either on the top or in the bobbin, I would limit its use in the bobbin. It tends to leave a stiff, harsh line of stitching, instead of the soft, up-and-down look of the cotton and nylon used together. I prefer to thread only the top of the machine with the nylon, and I use a 50 weight, 3-ply, 100% cotton sewing thread in the bobbin. The bobbin thread should match the lining fabric as closely as possible. This combination also eliminates snarling and breaking which can be very frustrating when nylon is used for both top and bobbin. If you do choose to use the nylon thread on the bobbin, the winding procedure is different than for sewing threads. Do not insert the thread through the thread guides and tension regulators as this causes the thread to stretch. Simply use your hand to guide the thread onto the bobbin as you run the machine.

You may find that your machine tension needs to be loosened on the top to allow for the weight difference of the two threads and for the high thread drag and stretchiness of the nylon thread. A size 80/12 needle is recommended, but you may find that the needle hole is too large and that the nylon thread does not fill the hole. A size 70/10 needle might be more appropriate for certain fabrics.

On one-color projects, such as whitework quilts, jackets, dresses, etc., the nylon might look too much like plastic when doing a lot of heavy quilting. In this case, try machine embroidery thread. This is a 2-ply, 100% cotton thread used for machine artwork. It is very fine and delicate, and it should not be substituted for the heavier sewing-weight thread used with the nylon. The embroidery thread is used when a great deal of stitching is being put into the fabric. It sews into the fabric flatter than heavier threads, and it leaves a beautiful texture. DMC® and Swiss-Metrosene both make machine embroidery threads. Look for size 50 or 60; 30 weight is usually too heavy.

FIG. 2.5 Cone holders

FIG. 2.6 Safety pin placement

As machine quilting becomes more popular, different threads are being used with great imagination. Don't overlook metallic and rayon threads to add sparkle and shine to your quilting. Experiment with different brands. There are good and bad threads for quilting. Your experience and testing will guide you to those that will work successfully in your machine. Brands to try include: Sulky® Rayon and Metallic, Madeira® metallic, Natesh® rayon, and Kanagawa metallic.

When using any of the speciality threads — nylon, rayon, or metallic — avoid putting the spool on the spool pin of the machine. These threads tend to be slick and come off the ends of the spools easily. Instead, use a cone holder that will hold the spool upright and off the machine. Sit the cone holder on the right side in back of the machine.

This keeps the thread from getting caught in the quilt. Use a closed safety pin, taped to the spool pin base, as a thread guide. As you thread the machine, insert it through the small hole in the safety pin first, then through the normal threading procedure. This will make the thread track from the same direction it would have if it were on the spool pin itself. Some machines have a thread guide attachment for this area, or they have one built into the area. Use this instead of the safety pin if your machine is so equipped (See Figure 2.5).

If you do not have a cone holder, a small jar (like an olive jar) works well as long as the jar does not allow the spool to fall over on its side (See Figure 2.6). It must be standing upright so that the thread comes off from the top. Again, use the safety pin thread guide system.

PART TWO

Preparing the Quilt

Choosing a Quilt Design

ONCE YOU HAVE COMPLETED the quilt top, press it extremely well using moisture or steam. Generally, you press the quilt top on the right side of the fabric. Be very careful about pressing all the way through the quilt piecing process to ensure a flat and true top when you are finished. Check the seam allowances to make sure that you do not have "accordions" in them. Accordions are the little folds or pleats that get pressed in when pressing from the wrong side of the fabric during construction. These pleats will create problems for you when machine quilting, especially ditch quilting. To avoid them, lay the piece on the ironing surface right side up. With the side of the iron, gently push the seam allowance to one side.

Once the quilt top is pressed smooth and flat, you are ready to mark the quilting patterns or lines onto its surface. If you are only ditch quilting, no marking is necessary. Not all quilting patterns and stencils are appropriate for beginning machine quilters. Continuous line patterns lend themselves easily to machine quilting. These patterns can be either simple or complicated in design, but their lines do not start and stop or weave in and out. Look for patterns that you can finger trace. Start in one spot, and trace through the entire design without starting or stopping or retracing any lines. Finger trace the designs below.

Another example of continuous line design would be the two feathers in Figure 3.2. The feather on the left is a traditional feather design. When hand quilting, it is easy to push the needle between the layers of the quilt to get from one spot to another, but we cannot do this with a sewing machine needle. There are two alternatives on the machine:

1) Lock off the threads at the beginning and end of every design line. This creates a sloppy looking back, and weakens the quilting.
2) Retrace the same line — exactly — to quilt the design and move from line to line without breaking the thread. This will take quite a bit of practice to achieve the accuracy needed.

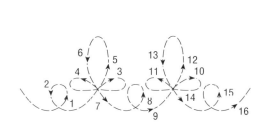

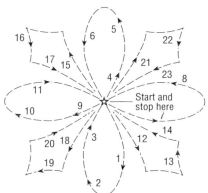

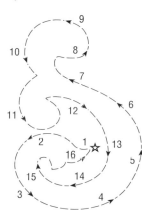

FIG. 3.1 Continuous quilting designs

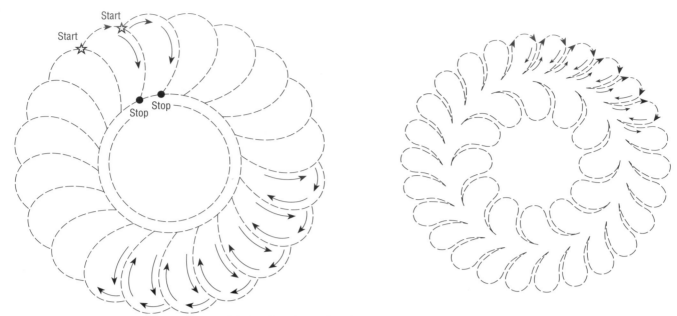

FIG. 3.2 Traditional and continuous feathered wreaths

The feather on the right can be worked continuously. Every petal has its own in-and-out stitching line, and you still can achieve a beautiful feather! You can do this design with very little practice.

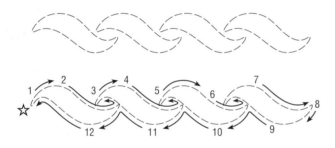

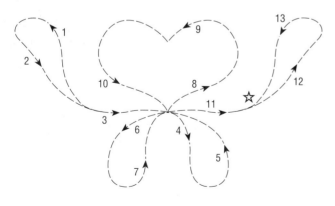

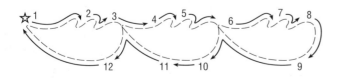

FIG. 3.3 Adapting designs to be continuous

Most designs that you find will not be continuous. But you can often still work with them if you can find a way to turn them into a continuous line system. Finger trace the designs in Figure 3.3 and see how the non-continuous lines can be done on the machine.

Sources for quilting designs can be found everywhere: coloring books, greeting cards, advertisements, folk art books, cut paper designs, as well as pre-cut stencils and over 20 titles of books devoted strictly to quilting patterns. Patterns are not normally available in the size you need. In the next section, I will discuss sizing the pattern to the quilt.

FIG. 3.4 Quilting design sources

Quilting Stencils

BECAUSE OF THE LIMITED VARIETY of precut stencils, seldom can you find the perfect design in the correct size for your project. Machine quilting requirements add to this dilemma, as few continuous line designs are precut. Here are some tricks for making your own stencils any size you need. These are very simple and inexpensive, and will provide a wealth of designs to draw from.

Your local printer can make the pattern the size you want with no trouble. Most copy shops have equipment that can enlarge or reduce the pattern without distortion. Once you get the pattern to the desired size, you have several options for making it usable.

DOUBLE-BLADED KNIFE METHOD

Most quilt shops carry DBK™ plastic. This is a very soft, clear plastic that is easily cut with an Exacto® knife. Use a double-bladed knife (also known as a Leaded Glass Pattern Cutter by Exacto) to cut the channels needed for the stencil. Begin by tracing the pattern lines onto the plastic with a permanent marker. Cut on either a rotary cutter mat or on a piece of glass. The knife cuts two parallel lines ⅛ inch apart, creating a channel. As you cut, lift the knife every so often to create the "bridges" necessary to keep the stencil from falling apart. After all the channels are cut, use a single-bladed knife or a small pair of scissors to clip out the ends of each channel. Now you have channel space for your

marking device. This method is especially useful for designs that have long, curvy lines where you can make a long, smooth cut. I have found that small, intricate patterns can be more difficult to cut with this method. After you have finished cutting the stencil, wipe off any permanent marker lines left on the plastic to avoid transferring ink onto your fabric.

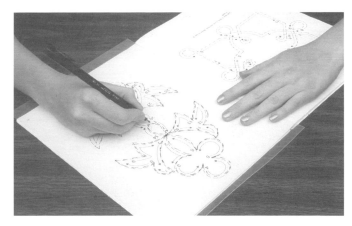

FIG. 4.1 Tracing onto plastic

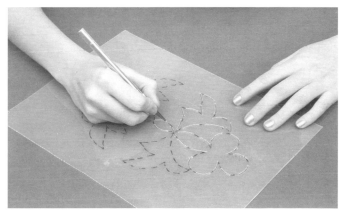

FIG. 4.2 Cutting with double-bladed knife

HOT PEN METHOD

Another fast method of making stencils involves using a hot pen. The instrument used is similar to a woodburning tool. NOTE: It is only safe to use this tool with Dupont Mylar®, not plastic. You will know mylar by the hard finish and the brittle feel and sound. Plastics emit toxic fumes when melted that are dangerous to your health.

While the pen is plugged in and heating up, trace your design onto the mylar with a permanent pen. You will need to curl the mylar up and off the surface of the table to achieve a clean cut with the pen. The instructions tell you to burn the mylar on a piece of glass, but the channel does not melt through clean. I have found it much more satisfactory to curl it up and work off the surface. Rest your forearm against the table to steady your hand. Insert the hot pen tip into the mylar at the beginning of a line. Slowly and evenly follow the line with the hot tip. When you need to stop for a bridge, pull the pen tip out straight, leave a space, then continue cutting the next line.

This tool is very helpful in making small, intricate patterns. Remove the bumps on the back of the stencil with a sanding block or a single-edge razor blade.

FIG. 4.3 Using hot pen

Both methods make durable, long-lasting stencils. Plan your cuts so that you get the longest line possible to speed your marking time. Long, straight or wavy lines can be cut up to 2½ inches before allowing for a bridge. Smaller areas and circles should have cuts of only ½ to 1 inch between bridges. Make sure you leave sufficient bridges to keep the stencil sturdy.

TULLE METHOD

If you need a design quickly and for short-term use, bridal illusion, tulle, is an option. This very fine, soft netting is used to make wedding veils and is readily available at fabric stores.

To use, lay the tulle on top of the copy of your design and pin. Trace the design onto the tulle using a permanent black felt-tip marker like a Sharpie® or a laundry marker. To prevent any residue from the marker from going onto the quilt when marking the quilt top, rinse the tulle out in soapy water. Press with a warm iron to dry.

FIG. 4.4 Tracing onto tulle

Place the tulle on the quilt top, pin in place, and use a liquid fabric marker, such as the water-soluable Mark-B-Gone™ or an air erasable pen to transfer your pattern. (A liquid marker is preferable.) As you are tracing the lines on the tulle, the liquid ink goes into the holes of the tulle and leaves dots on your quilt top, marking your quilting line. When the tulle is removed, the entire pattern is on the top, ready to quilt.

FIG. 4.5 Tracing through tulle onto quilt top

This is a very simple and practical way to mark designs without having any bridges. You do not need to guess where the line should be at the bridges. However, water-soluble marking tools do not work on dark fabrics, dry pencils tend to tear the tulle, and chalk powders brush off too easily.

TEAR-AWAY METHOD

There is an alternate method for marking problem fabrics such as velvet, lamé, satins, sateens, silks, etc. Use Tear-Away, a very soft, paper-type product that tears cleanly away from stitching. If you are doing a large project, sew pieces of Tear-Away together to get the needed size. This method can be used on very small areas like pockets on velvet jackets, or it can be used on large projects like whole-cloth quilts.

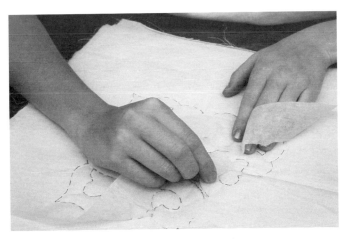

FIG. 4.6   Tear-Away method

Mark your pattern onto the Tear-Away. When putting the quilt layers together, position the Tear-Away over the quilt top, so you have four layers to your sandwich. Then quilt through all four layers. After quilting, gently remove the Tear-Away from the stitching. This is not a speed technique, just a safe one that protects fragile fabrics. Tear-Away comes in either soft or crisp.

RUG CANVAS METHOD

Crosshatch quilting is very attractive and can usually be done easily on the machine. However, it is not easy to mark on the quilt top. Use a latch-hook rug canvas to make your stencil. Because it is an even-weave fabric, there are squares woven in. By marking permanent lines in a grid on the canvas,

you automatically have a perfect grid. (Use a permanent ink felt-tip marker such as the Sharpie.) Follow the squares in a straight line to keep the line straight and the angle accurate. By counting the number of holes between each line, you can keep the spacing consistent. The grid lines can be marked as far apart as you like. The grid can be diagonal, straight, double diagonal, one straight and one diagonal, etc.

FIG. 4.7   Marking grid onto rug canvas

To mark the quilt top, place the canvas on the quilt in the proper position and pin if necessary. Using a felt-tip fabric marker, such as Mark-B-Gone, start with one line and make a dot with the marker in the hole that the line goes through. Continue doing this up the length of the line. Now come back down on the next line, making a dot in each hole you come to along the line. Do all of one direction first, then repeat the process for the other direction. When the canvas is removed, you will have dotted lines that are perfect in spacing as well as angle.

Rug canvas, available at craft stores that sell latch-hook rug supplies, comes by the yard so you can make your stencil any size you need. For borders, the canvas can be cut the width of the border, in an "L" shape to accommodate the corner and ½ of the

FIG. 4.8   Marking onto quilt top

length of each side border. This way you only need to align the canvas four times, and the corners are marked perfectly. Rug canvas stencils are reusable many times.

LIGHT BOX

Another alternative to cutting stencils is the use of a light box for tracing. This method is especially useful for large projects where much time would be needed to prepare stencils or where the quilting pattern is very detailed.

You can set up a light box system inexpensively by using a lamp and a table that expands. Expand the table to create an opening, and cover the open area with a sheet of glass. Place a lamp without the shade on the floor below the glass. Higher wattage bulbs make it easier to trace onto dark fabrics.

Trace your quilting pattern onto white butcher paper using a bold black line. Tape the pattern onto the glass. Turn the lamp on, allowing the light to

shine through the glass and paper. Position the quilt top over the paper. The fabric becomes translucent, enabling you to see through the fabric to the marked lines. Trace the lines onto the quilt top, repositioning when necessary.

PIN PRICK METHOD

Antique quilts are excellent sources for quilting designs, often originals not readily found elsewhere. To copy a pattern from an antique quilt, place a sheet of butcher paper over cardboard, cork or carpeting. Lay the antique quilt on top of the paper. With a sharp pin or needle, prick through the quilt and the paper as you follow the quilting lines. This method of transferring the pattern causes minimal damage to the quilt and eliminates the risk of making lines on the quilt by surface tracing.

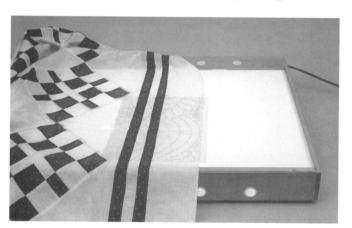

FIG. 4.9 Light box

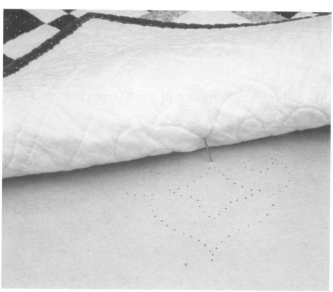

FIG. 4.10 Pin pricking to obtain design

Sizing a Quilting Design to Fit a Border

BORDER STENCILS AND PATTERNS seldom automatically fit within the borders of a quilt. There is a simple mathematical way to figure the adjustments needed to make a design fit a given area. Work through the following example using a quilt that measures 84 by 96 inches. Figure each side separately. Carefully measure the finished edge of one

side of your quilt. For this example use the 96-inch side.

1) Measure your quilting design from the outermost corner to the beginning of the first pattern repeat. See Figure 4.11a. Make a note of this measurement. This example measures 4¾ inches.

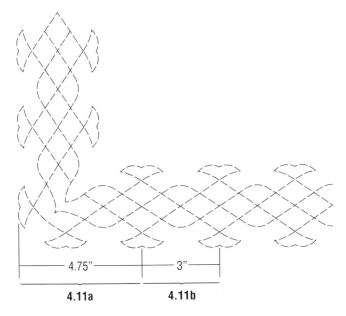

—— 4.75" —— ——— 3" ———
4.11a   **4.11b**

FIG. 4.11a Measurement of outermost corner
FIG. 4.11b Measurement of pattern repeat

2) Double that measurement to accommodate both corners of that side.

Example: 4.75 inches + 4.75 inches = 9.5 inches

3) Subtract the amount in step 2 from the border length.

Example: 96 inches – 9.5 inches = 86.5 inches

4) Into this measurement, divide the length of one pattern repeat. See Figure 4.11b.

Example: $\dfrac{86.5 \text{ inches}}{3 \text{ inches}} = 28.83$

This number tells you how many repeats are needed to fill the border space.

NOTE: You will need to decide whether it would be easier to shorten or lengthen the design when the answer is not a round number. In this example, it would be easier to round up to 29 repeats.

5) Multiply the pattern repeat measurement by the number of repeats needed.

Example: 29 repeats × 3 inches = 87 inches

6) Using the two measurements that you got from steps 3 and 5, subtract the smaller from the larger. If step 3 is larger, the pattern repeat will need to be lengthened. If step 5 is larger, the pattern repeat will need to be shortened.

Example: 87 inches – 86.5 inches = .5 inches

7) Divide the answer from step 6 by the number of repeats needed for the border. This number tells you how much adjustment needs to be made to each pattern repeat.

Example: $\dfrac{.5 \text{ inches}}{29 \text{ inches}} = .017$

In this example, each pattern repeat will need to be made shorter by .017 inches. This adjustment can be made on the stencil if you are cutting your own, or on the quilt as you mark the pattern.

PREPARING THE QUILT FOR MARKING

Registration lines, used for placement accuracy, need to be marked onto the quilt's surface before marking any designs. Pre-cut stencils are not always straight on the plastic so it is up to you to determine the actual size of the design and how it should sit on the quilt. The size you need to determine is the actual area of the design itself, not the plastic.

BLOCK OR FILL DESIGNS

For block stencils, you need to find the exact center of the pattern, as well as the center points on the outside edges of the design. See Figure 4.12. Measure the quilt block so that you know where the center points of the block are, both in the middle of the square and on the outside edges. See Figure 4.13. Align the stencil registration lines with the markings on the block. This will assure a centered and well-placed design.

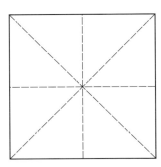

FIG. 4.12 Registration lines for quilt block

FIG. 4.13 Registration lines for stencil

BORDERS AND CORNERS

Below are instructions for setting the registration lines on the border and in the corners. Chapter 5 tells which marking tools to use.

1) Mark a 45° angle line in each corner.

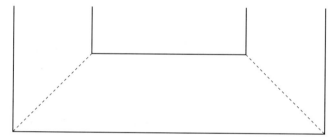

FIG. 4.14 Diagonal corner registration lines

2) If there are no seams, draw a line with a ruler that extends the border seamlines across the width of the border on all sides.

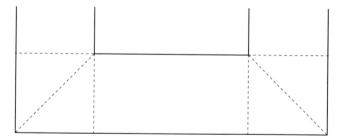

FIG. 4.15 Corner registration lines

3) Find the midpoint of the border width. Measure from the corner of the quilt top (the border

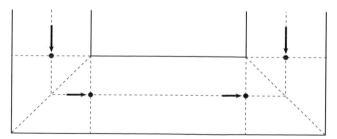

FIG. 4.16 Finding mid-points

seam) to the edge of the border. Subtract ¼-inch seam allowance from this measurement. Mark a dot at each corner on the lines drawn in the previous step. Connect the width midpoints with a line the length of each border.

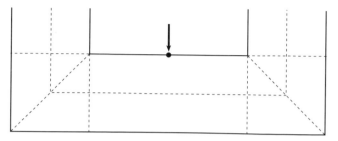

FIG. 4.17 Finding border length mid-point

4) Measure the length of each border to find the midpoint. Make a mark on the border seam.

PREPARING THE STENCIL

Mark the registration lines directly onto the stencil with a permanent pen.

1) Draw a line to show the 45° angle of the corner.
2) Find the center of the design and draw a line the length of the stencil.

FIG. 4.18 Registration marks on border stencil

These lines will lie directly on top of the quilt registration lines. By having the register set, the stencils will always line up with the borders and turn the corners accurately.

When all the register lines are set, you will be ready to mark the quilt top. The next chapter will help you choose marking pencils and pens for your quilts.

Marking Tools

THERE ARE MANY MARKING TOOLS available and it is the quilter's responsibility to make sure that the marker chosen is safe on the fabric used. When choosing a marker, always consider the method and ease of removing the marking lines. NOTE: The same tools do not always work the same on different projects.

MARKING PENCILS

Traditionally, a graphite pencil has been used to draw directly onto the quilt top. Do not use a #2 soft lead pencil because the cotton fabric tends to absorb the line and seldom releases it totally. A #4H hard lead engineering pencil works well. The point stays sharp and leaves a very light line. It is suitable for light solids, muslin, and white fabrics.

There are a variety of markers available for light and print fabrics. Below I have listed those that are satisfactory for machine quilting. Not all pencils used by hand quilters are successful for machine work.

A brand that gives excellent results is Caran D'Ache Supracolor® I. These are watercolor pencils which are easily removed from fabric, but the only colors that I would use are white, gold, and silver. Do not use the true colors, as the pigment can cause problems. These pencils leave a dark, bold line by using a very light touch so the lead is not being ground into the fabric. Marks wipe off easily with a damp cloth. Dixon Washout Cloth Markers are very good for prints and colors. They are available in red, green, and blue. The red and green are especially helpful when marking on darker prints.

A word of warning about the chalk wheels that have been so popular in the past few years. In many cases the dye in the chalk does not wash out of the fabric or the thread used in machine quilting. Always test the red, blue, and yellow chalks. Yellow can be especially troublesome because the sulfur in it tends to be permanent in fabrics. The white has no dye, so it is perfectly safe.

There are several good white markers that can be used on dark fabrics. A white charcoal pencil called Charcoal White®, from USA General, is very good, as is the white pastel pencil from West Germany called Carb-Othello®. Neither of these have additives that can cause problems on fabrics. Be careful about using white dressmaker's chalk pencils because the high amount of wax in them can be very difficult to remove. They are made to mark on the inside of garments, not on the right side.

New marking products are always being found for use on quilts. General Pencil Co. has pencils new to quilters, the Multi-Pastel Chalks®, that work very well, as does the new Berol Karismacolor® Graphite Aquarelle®, which is a water-soluble graphite pencil. We've found the medium lead to work best. Keep an eye out for other new products that would be applicable to your quilting needs.

NOTE: Always pretest all marking devices you have chosen before marking the quilt top. Because of the variety of sizings and finishes on fabrics, as well as dye properties, each fabric can react differently to various marking tools. A pencil may be safe on every fabric in the quilt except one, but you won't know that until it has ruined that fabric if you do not pretest. Never take anyone's word for the reliability of a marking tool on your fabric.

The test is simple and should be done whether you prewash the fabrics or not. Gather scraps of every fabric in the quilt that you need to mark with a design or line. Have a variety of marking tools that will show on each color. Mark lines on each fabric, making the line as dark as you need to see it readily.

NOTE: This is where machine quilters can get into trouble with marking tools. Hand quilters can work with very faint lines, because they generally have good light and no vision obstructions. The machine, however, has a poor lighting system, leaving us with shadows and dark spots. We also have limited vision because of the machine head. This makes it necessary to have darker lines. Making dark lines by pressing hard with any pencil can spell trouble!

Once you have the lines marked, take a damp cloth and rub gently with the grain of the fabric to remove the lines. If the line comes off easily, the marking tool is a good choice for that one particular fabric. Do this test with each fabric sample. You may need a variety of tools for marking the various fabrics in your quilt top.

Some pencils do not come off easily but can be removed when laundering. If you plan to launder the quilt, pretest the markers either when you prewash the fabrics or by using soapy water on your samples.

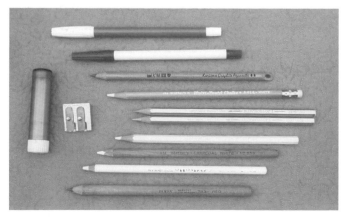

FIG. 5.1 Various marking pencils

WASH-OUT LIQUID MARKING PENS

Felt-tip liquid markers used in quiltmaking have received a lot of bad publicity. These are better known as Mark-B-Gone, Fade-Away™, etc. They usually have blue or purple ink that is removable with water.

When they first appeared on the market a few years ago, they were "miracle" markers, but time has shown them to be potentially dangerous to fabric unless used properly. These pens were developed for dressmaking, and instructions were not originally included. Quilters began using them without removing them sufficiently, causing the lines to discolor and become permanent. The chemical, if left in the fabric, can weaken and break down the fibers. The lines can be heat set and become permanent if ironed or exposed to high heat while in the fabric. Be especially careful of the purple air-erasable pens. These lines totally disappear from light sensitivity and humidity. However, the chemical is still in the fabric and will cause permanent and unsightly damage to the quilt if not removed thoroughly.

Remove the chemical after the quilting is finished. Completely submerge the quilt into cold, clear water. Do not use soap because its ingredients can also set the lines. Soak the quilt until all the lines have totally disappeared. Then launder it in a neutral detergent such as Orvus Paste® and warm water to remove the chemical from the fibers. Once this has been done, you will not have a problem with the felt-tip pens. To pretest, mark the lines onto scraps of the designated fabrics, soak in cool, clear water until the lines disappear, then wash in soapy water. Rinse, then iron dry with a hot iron. If the lines do not reappear in any way, you are safe with that fabric.

Visit your local quilt shop, craft supply store, or art supply store for a good selection of marking pencils and pens. Try a variety of tools and pretest them all before marking your quilt top.

The Inside Story – Batting

ONE OF THE MOST OVERLOOKED, least understood and least discussed products in quiltmaking is batting. This key ingredient can either enhance a quilt's beauty or it can detract from and distort the quilt's surface. There is no one batting that is appropriate for every quilt. Quilters must consider factors such as desired surface texture, weight, warmth, loft, drape, shrinkage, fiber content, washability and wearability, bearding properties, ease of needling, etc. All of these factors play as important a role in the quilt's overall appearance as do fabric choices, design piecing and appliqué techniques used.

Machine quilting adds another dimension to your batting choices. As a beginner, you want to use a batting that will cooperate with you and your machine to eliminate distortion and thus frustration. As your skills improve, so will your willingness to take on more unruly battings. The fiber content, manufacturing process, and loft of each different batting will affect the manageability and success of the quilting process.

There are many excellent battings on the market, but there is no one perfect batt. I will enumerate the products available and tell you the pros and cons of each. I will divide the batting products by fiber content and give you guidelines on spacing the quilting lines, and laundering. Keep in mind that machine quilting techniques are very different from hand quilting techniques: Battings that are difficult to hand needle are suddenly excellent choices for the machine.

I suggest that you obtain samples of every batting available and every new batting product that appears on the market. Layer the samples, quilt them according to the guidelines given in this book, wash and dry them like mini-quilts, and see what happens to the batting. Measure them before washing, and again after they are dry to see whether the batting shrinks and how the fabric reacts to it in the washing process. Do these samples using both pre-washed and non-prewashed fabric for each batting. This gives you two samples to compare, and lets you decide which fabric treatment is appropriate for the quilt you have in mind. Go one step farther and wash these samples every week in the family wash to see how well the batting holds up.

Natural Fibers

THE MOST COMMONLY USED natural fibers in quilt-making are cotton and wool. Research and development in the United States have brought us excellent new, natural fiber products for use in quilts. With some basic understanding of the fibers and their characteristics and behaviors, you can enjoy using these battings in your quilts with excellent results. And, as evidenced by our antique quilts, natural fibers stand the test of time.

COTTON

Cotton battings were first manufactured in the 1850s, and today's battings are similarly manufactured. Harvested cotton bolls are sent through a cotton gin to separate the cotton fibers from the seed. This process also removes foreign matter such as dirt, twigs, leaves and parts of the bolls. Next, the resulting fiber, or cotton lint, is packed into large bales and sent to a spinning mill. At the mill, the cotton is opened to remove any remaining impurities. This process consists of a beating mechanism which loosens the cotton. The opened fibers are blown against a perforated drum, and the impurities are removed. The shorter fibers also pass through the drum leaving the longer fibers to be rolled into a sheet. The result of this process is what we use for batting. It is finished with a glazing to help prevent shifting and lumping.

There are three excellent cotton battings on the market now. Mountain Mist®, a division of The Stearns Company, and Fairfield Processing are manufacturing cotton and cotton blend battings that have a variety of characteristics that fill machine quilter's needs perfectly:

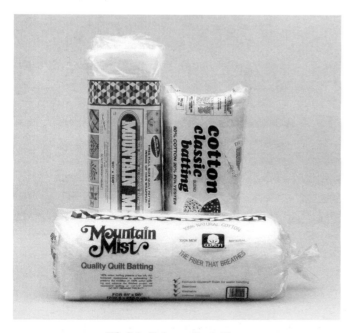

FIG. 6.1 Various cotton battings

1) The cotton fibers of the batting stick to the quilt top and backing fabrics, preventing the shifting, slipping, distortion, and stretching that occurs with polyester battings under the machine. This allows us to pin baste less, and eliminates puckers, tucks, and ruffled borders on our machine-quilted quilts. This is the major reason for a beginning machine quilter to use cotton battings.

2) Because the fibers do stick together and the batting is much thinner, when the quilt is rolled to go through the sewing machine, the roll is much smaller.

3) Now king-sized, cotton batted quilts can be quilted in one piece. The roll stays rolled while going through the machine, and takes up much less space.

4) Cotton battings shrink some when washed. The shrinkage is at the same rate as the cotton fabrics used in the quilt. (Avoid using fabric blends because the quilt fabric and the batt will shrink at different rates.) Shrinkage can be beneficial for several reasons. It gives the quilt an aged look which is desirable when trying to replicate an antique quilt. Also, when you are just learning to machine quilt, there are glitches in your work that you want to camouflage. The shrinkage of the batting, when the quilt is first laundered, causes puckering around the stitching. This makes it difficult to tell how the quilt was quilted, and hides many of the little problem areas. This way, you can learn to machine quilt on quilts, instead of wasting hours of precious time on muslin samples.

5) Cotton is extremely comfortable to sleep under. Cotton breathes, allowing excess heat to escape. Thus you are never too hot under cotton quilts. For this reason, it is excellent for baby quilts. Quilts with cotton batts are not quite as warm as polyester or wool, but for many, polyester and wool are too hot. Cotton is also less dangerous around heat sources, as it is not combustible and does not melt like polyester. It can also be sanitized.

6) Cotton endures. Even with hard use, cotton ages gracefully, becoming softer and more cuddly with age.

7) Pure cotton battings do not beard like polyester battings.

Mountain Mist 100% Natural Cotton

Mountain Mist has been producing this batting, or one very similar, for over 100 years. This batting is the only one on the market that gives quilts an antique appearance of softness and puckering most characteristic of the quilts from the 1920s and 1930s. It is appropriate for the quilt tops made from the marvelous reproduction fabrics of the late 1800s, and early 1900s. If you put polyester into these quilt tops, they do not look old, but fluffy instead. Batting choices are critical when trying to achieve an aged look.

This batting will need to be quilted no further apart than 1 inch. The package suggests ¼- to ½-inch spacing. That is a tremendous amount of quilting by hand, but it only takes a matter of hours for the machine quilter. Most hand quilters dislike this batting because it is hard to needle. The machine needle has the opposite reaction. It can penetrate almost anything, so the thickness of the fibers is not an issue. Because the batting and fabric stick together, the machine presser foot does not feel any resistance or drag from the batting. It glides over the fabric and designs. Because of this, I strongly suggest that you use this batting for your first larger project, and your success rate will climb.

100% Natural will shrink more than the other cotton products, often up to 2 inches in length and width when the quilt is washed and dried. It is not finished with any chemicals to bond it together — a natural starch is used to secure the fibers together for ease in handling. The starch is washed away when the quilt is laundered, so do not presoak this batting!

To counteract the size loss and still get the look and feel you desire, I suggest that you again work with the samples mentioned previously. Work with both prewashed and non-prewashed fabric samples. Layer the samples and quilt them at least every inch. Cut to a specific size (I would suggest at least 12 inches to 14 inches), serge or zigzag the edges, and launder as you would the quilt. Drying the quilt in the dryer will give you more shrinkage than air drying flat, so if you intend to use your dryer, make sure that you do the same for your samples. For your own information, you might want to do two sets of samples. Dry one set in a warm dryer, the other flat. Once dry, measure the samples again.

You can find the percentage of shrinkage by using this formula:

$$\% \text{ shrinkage} = \frac{\text{original measurement} - \text{final measurement}}{\text{original measurement}} \times 100$$

When prewashing yardage, especially if you dry in a dryer, you will see a fair amount of shrinkage in your yard goods. However, if you cut new fabric into small pieces, sew it together into a quilt top, quilt to batting and backing fabric, then wash it, you will notice negligible shrinkage. This is because the fabrics are stabilized by the quilting. Again, test this for yourself and see what happens. Get comfortable with the products you are working with. Quilting is not dressmaking, and the fabrics behave differently in each respective application.

If you do choose to use prewashed fabrics, the shrinkage of the batting after washing can cause the batting to split and tear within the quilting lines. Closer quilting (½ inch) may alleviate this. I personally never prewash my fabrics when working with this batting.

Mountain Mist Blue Ribbon

Blue Ribbon is a relatively new batting on the market in which Mountain Mist has tried to correct some of the hand quilting drawbacks of their 100% Natural batting. It is still 100% cotton, but a bonding agent has been applied to the fiber to give it stability and strength. This process creates a batting of 100% cotton fiber, which shrinks very little. Run the tests given so you know how much shrinkage you can expect. Blue Ribbon has a thinner and flatter appearance than the 100% Natural. It is not a substitute for 100% Natural, just an alternative.

Blue Ribbon can be quilted at 1½- to 2-inch intervals instead of 1 inch or closer. This allows you to use a cotton batting in a quilt that you do not wish to quilt so heavily, while retaining the comfort and beauty of cotton. It is equally easy to work with on the machine. You will not get the advantage of puckering when washed, even with unwashed fabrics. However, if you prefer to work with only prewashed fabrics or if you have an extensive collection of prewashed fabrics, you can now use a pure cotton batting with them. Blue Ribbon will not tear or split when laundered if quilting distances are within given guidelines. Again, do not presoak this batting!

Both 100% Natural and Blue Ribbon break down as a powder, eliminating bearding. They are both excellent choices for working with black or other dark fabrics where bearding is unsightly.

Fairfield Processing Corporation Cotton Classic®

Cotton Classic is not a pure 100% cotton batting. It is made from blending 80% cotton fibers with 20% polyester fibers, forming a web, and bonding the web with a resin to keep the fibers together. This batting is similar to, yet very different from the Mountain Mist cottons.

NOTE: This is the only cotton-type batting that can be presoaked. Fairfield recommends presoaking if you want to soften the batting to ease needling, a problem when hand quilting. Cotton Classic is hard to hand needle without presoaking, but it is not necessary to presoak for machine work, except when shrinkage is a consideration. Sometimes the batting will shrink, other times it will not, so you should do a shrinkage test on every new batt you purchase. Then, if you want shrinkage to be a part of your quilt's appearance and the batt you have tested doesn't shrink, you can substitute one that will, and not be disappointed. On the other hand, if you make a garment, and shrinkage is not desirable, you can presoak the batting.

Cotton Classic can be quilted at 2- to 3-inch intervals. This allows you to use a cotton-type batting in items that before couldn't handle cotton because of the close quilting requirements. This batting is excellent in garments, as it breathes and adds no bulk or puff. One drawback that needs to be pointed out about this batt is that it does have the potential to beard on black and dark fabrics.

To presoak the batting, fill the washer with tepid water (no detergents or soaps), unfold the batting, and gently push it into the water. Do not agitate. Let the batt rest in the water for 5 to 10 minutes, then spin the water out using the gentle spin cycle. Dry in the dryer on air or fluff for 15 to 20 minutes, until just dry. Handle the batt carefully during this process.

Cotton Classic has an antique, soft, textured appearance if used with new fabric without prewashing the batt. It is not a substitute for either 100% Natural or Blue Ribbon, but it is an alternative. Mark your samples with indelible ink so that you have a permanent record of the differences in appearance for each product.

All of the above battings come in queen-size only. If a larger batt is needed, cut a straight edge on both pieces, butt together, and secure with a 3-step zigzag on the machine. Do not overlap the edges.

NOTE: I have found that the color of the fabric used for the quilt top and back can be affected greatly by the batting chosen. If you are working with light prints or light solids like parchment, ecru, white, or muslin, watch what happens to the color of the fabric when different battings are placed between the layers. Polyester, being a transparent product, lets the light go through the quilt, lessening color density. Whites and cream colors turn slightly gray from this dilution of color. On the other hand, if you place a cotton batt between the same layers, the light cannot pass through because it is opaque. The fabric will retain the color saturation.

I suggest that you keep sample squares of different battings to test the effects they have on your quilt. Cotton battings allow you to have a dark backing on a light quilt, whereas polyester lets the color soak through, distorting the color of the quilt top. Medium and dark colors are not affected by this, but lighter-weight and light-colored fabrics are definitely affected by batting choices. Keep in mind that cotton battings are not appropriate for all quilts.

COTTON FLANNEL

Flannel was very popular in antique quilts. Exquisite tiny hand stitches were made possible because of the thinness of the cloth.

Often overlooked today, cotton flannel yardage or flannel bed sheets are an excellent batting to be used in summer-weight quilts. Flannelette is brushed on both sides, making it thicker. Because flannel is a woven fabric, as opposed to the non-woven fibers of batting, quilting distances can be even greater. Consider using flannel in baby quilts, lap robes, garments, wall quilts, etc. It can be used either as a batting or the back and batting all in one. Prewashing is advised as flannel tends to shrink more than broadcloth fabrics because of the lower thread count.

WOOL

Wool batting is starting to see a revived interest from quiltmakers. Wool was the fiber of choice when warmth and durability were needed, and we now use it for a substitute for polyester when natural fibers are desirable. The comfort of wool is universally recognized as superior to man-made (plastic) fibers. It is very warm and lofty without being heavy and wiry.

Wool has characteristics that no other fiber provides. First, the wool fiber has built-in crimp, giving it bounce and loft that allows it to always return to its original shape. Wool has a recovery rate from compression of 95% which is better than any other fiber (polyester averages 73% depending on the type of polyester fiber treatment used). This resiliency provides long-lasting beauty and warmth.

Wool also has a natural bonding ability that polyester does not have. The fiber is composed of scales overlapping one another, and once separated by shaking or airing, they will reattach to each other in a new position, allowing the fullness to be re-created. Polyester does not have this ability. Airing wool quilts and comforters twice a year restores loft and fullness to the fiber.

Wool breathes, allowing our skin to remain warm, yet dry. It moderates temperature, so that you never get too hot or too cold sleeping under it. The wool can also absorb up to 33% of its own weight in moisture without feeling damp, as opposed to 4% for synthetics. This makes it a perfect quilt for a damp, cold climate. Polyester tends to become clammy when damp.

Wool batting is made from scoured wool. Thorough scouring removes excess lanolin. The wool is then carded and combed. Combing removes plant and insect particles as well as the shorter, coarser wool fibers. Carding and combing produces unspun wool. To make the batt, it is then opened or "plucked" apart into fluffy fiber. The higher quality of wool used, the softer and fluffier the batt will be. Quilters have the option of using an "opened" (web) wool batting or a needle-punched wool batting. The opened batt, used for comforters, is fluffier, with loose fiber. Needle-punched wool is made to be quilted.

COMBED AND OPENED WOOL BATTING

These batts are generally homemade or manufactured by small businesses. Order samples of these batts before purchasing them in any quantity. Some are of beautiful quality, and some are dirty and hardly suitable for quilting.

Encase these combed and opened wool batts in a cheesecloth covering before putting them into quilts. Wool fiber will migrate easily through to the surface of the fabric if not contained.

Cheesecloth comes 44 inches wide, and I prefer to use 40-gauge weave. Apply it to both sides of the wool batt and baste every 3 to 4 inches using long, loose stitches with a tapestry needle. Finish the edges of the cheescloth so that the batt is totally encased. Now the batting is ready for the layering process. Once this is done, you can quilt every 3 to 5 inches without worry. Quilting distance depends on how you will clean the quilt. Quilt more closely if you plan to wash the quilt, and quilt further apart if you plan to dry-clean.

NEEDLE-PUNCHED WOOL

Taos Mountain Wool Works is a company that produces a superior quality wool batting using the needle-punch process. A uniform quality, Merino-type wool is used. A long, soft wool fiber intended for worsted fabrics, it gives the batt a light weight and a superior drape.

The fiber is scoured, carded, combed and plucked into a fluffy fiber web. This web is fed into needle-punching equipment. The needles, which have barbs protruding from the shaft, move through the layer of fibers, and the barbs push the fibers into distorted and tangled arrangements. The web is contained by metal plates above and below so the fibers cannot be pulled or pushed beyond the web layer. As the web moves slowly through the machine, the needles punch as many times as desired for the end product. This process reduces the amount of fiber migration common to wool batts. It also reduces air circulation, making the batt very warm relative to its thickness.

The manufacturers suggest lightly steaming the surfaces of the batt with a steam iron before using. This reduces the risk of migrating fibers. I have done this and still found migrating to be a problem. I suggest that you also encase the batt in cheesecloth. Needle-punched wool batts can be quilted or tied, approximately 3 to 5 inches apart. Quilt closer if cheesecloth is not used.

It is recommended that wool quilts be dry-cleaned to prevent shrinkage, but vacuuming, as well as airing on a cloudy, breezy day, is usually sufficient for cleaning. Wool naturally repels dirt. Keep the surface fabrics protected from soiling by putting your wool quilt between a sheet and another blanket. This eliminates any washing problems. If you do decide to wash your quilt, use only tepid wash and rinse water. Use a neutral detergent, such as Orvus Paste. Handle as you would your very finest cashmere sweater.

Synthetic Fibers

ONCE POLYESTER BATTING WAS INTRODUCED on the market, quilting took on a new look. Quilters liked its ease of handling, warmth, strength and low cost. Beginning quilters found success in their attempts without extensive hand quilting. By the late 1970s, polyester was the predominant batting used by quilters, and new quilters were not given any choices. The idea that the batting should complement the quilt was lost for a number of years. Like natural fibers, synthetics have both desirable and undesirable qualities.

A look at how the batts are manufactured will explain why they behave the way they do and help guide you through the maze of products on the market. The battings available for use in quiltmaking can vary in web formation, the bonding technique used, and the curing or drying process.

Polyester batts are made using either the oriented web or random web (air-lay) process. Oriented webs are made on conventional carding equipment. The fibers are metered and uniformly distributed on a moving belt. Several webs may be superimposed to obtain the desired thickness. The fibers can all be parallel to each other (lengthwise) or placed at right angles to one another by building layers of fibers. When all layers are lengthwise, the web is strong lengthwise, but weak crosswise. With the right-angle fiber layers, strength is found in both directions. The fibers are bonded together either through an adhesive applied to the surface (glazing) or by the addition of heat sensitive fibers which help seal the final fabric as they soften and fuse with other fibers when heated. This process is characteristic of Mountain Mist Glazene® process polyester batting, both regular weight and Quilt-Light®.

Random webs are made on special machines which suspend the fibers in a rapidly moving airstream. They are then blown or forced onto a continuously moving belt where the web is formed. The fiber arrangement is random, and the web has relatively uniform characteristics. This process is common for what we call "bonded batting" and is characteristic of many brands, including Fairfield Processing's Extra Loft®, Low Loft®, Hi Loft® and Hobbs Bonded Fibers Poly-Down® battings.

The bonding is achieved either through the application of an adhesive binder, the softening of some fibers in the fiber mix by heat, or the use of solvents which chemically soften some of the fibers so that they will bind the fiber mat together. The mat is stable after the solvent has been removed.

The final stage for both processes is drying and curing. Drying devices include hot-air ovens, heated cans, infrared lights and high-frequency electrical equipment. The choice depends on the particular binding agent.

When examining the characteristics of either of these methods, carefully consider the end use of the quilt, as well as the quilting distance to be used. Choose only premium, packaged batts that are intended for quilts. Many polyester batts are too stiff and thick for quilts, and are intended for craft purposes, upholstery, and commercial uses.

Mountain Mist produces an oriented web batt of 100% polyester fiber that is finished with a Glazene finish. This process gives a quilt different characteristics than does a bonded batt. Because the bonding is achieved by applying the resin to only the surface of the web, the inside fibers are loose and free. This can create some drawbacks where bearding is concerned; however, the more quilting that is put into the batting, the less it tends to beard. Very close, dense stitching can be done without the characteristic stiffness that most polyester batts show. It also allows you to quilt very closely in one area and further apart in another without distortion.

Suggested distance for spacing quilting stitches is from ¼ inch to a maximum of 2 inches to 2½ inches apart. The more space between stitch lines, the more shifting and bearding is likely.

Mountain Mist polyester batts have the appearance and loft of cotton. This allows the quiltmaker to have the somewhat antique look of cotton without its disadvantages: shrinkage, weight, and the need for extremely close quilting. It is also very easy to work with on the machine. It is not springy and it does not drag under the needle as the thicker polyesters do.

We have been told over the last decade that bonded batting was the only safe batting to use, but no explanation of "safe" was ever given. Thus, it was put into every quilt made, with little or no consideration of its weak points. We were also told that it could be quilted 6 inches to 8 inches apart, which we are now seeing is a major error. Quilts made in the past 15 years with polyester batting are aging poorly.

The bonding process was invented to artificially add loft to the batt, but there is no more actual fiber in a one-pound thick batt than there is in a one-pound flatter batt. Therefore, over time, the bonded batts will lose their loft. Further, a process of stretching and roping occurs as the resins and air space break down. Roping is evidenced by the migration and attraction of the synthetic fibers joining together and creating a firm mass of fiber. This "rope" then twists slightly, leaving small ridges in the batting. Purchased comforters do this after several washings. It can be caused by poor quality product, under-quilting, or both. On the other hand, bonded battings offer warmth with little weight, the ability to be quilted up to 4 inches apart, and the puffy look that enhances so many quilts.

Often quilters shop for batting by weight, such as a 3- or 4-ounce batting. Most of the weight of a batt comes from its bonding additives. Because every company uses a different bonding agent in varying amounts to bond the fibers together, it is not possible to compare products by weight. The weight can also be affected by the fiber content and the thickness of the fiber used when layering, making the thickness of the batt the prime consideration, not the weight.

Needle-punched polyester batting is also available for use in quilting. Because it tends to be denser and stiffer than the other polyesters, it is desirable for quilted projects, such as wall quilts, placemats, garments, pillows, etc., but not for quilts.

There are different ways to produce needle-punched batting. The batt is laid with five or more layers across the width of the belt. One method runs the batt through a machine with rows of needles that pound and compress the product to a uniform thickness. It comes out with approximately 10% of the original loft. Another method uses barbed needles that curl and intertwine the fibers into a dense batt. The third method sends the batt of thermoplastic fibers through a machine using hot needles. The needles melt the parts of the fibers that they touch, causing them to fuse together to form a more stable batt. Some brands of needle-punched batting are Traditional™ from Fairfield Processing corporation, Pellon® Fleece, and Thermore® from Hobbs. These batts are more likely to beard at first because the fibers on top are not interlocked. Washing should eventually wear the loose fibers off, making the batt more stable.

The bearding syndrome of polyester battings must be taken seriously because once it starts, there is no cure. The process often does not begin until the resin breaks down from usage, and it can last up to three years. Choose good quality, high thread-count fabrics. If lower quality fabrics or blends are used, expect bearding to be a problem. To camouflage bearding on dark fabrics, Hobbs Bonded Fibers has produced a charcoal grey batting, Poly-Down-DK®.

One of the ways manufacturers are trying to improve synthetic battings is by using "slick," hollow-core fibers. The theory is that the slick fibers will not stick together as badly as regular fibers, cutting down on the compression rate, or loss of loft. They are also supposed to reduce static and bearding. Because they use softer fibers, they provide more warmth. Hobbs Bonded Fibers has produced a batting called Poly-Down that is made of these slick fibers, 100% Loftguard® Polyester.

Consumers need to be aware that all synthetic battings are made of thermoplastic fibers which are very heat sensitive. This could pose a threat if the finished product is to be exposed to direct heat. The fiber will melt instantly, and the melting spreads rapidly. Also, resins and bonding agents are chemicals that are potentially combustible. These factors need to be considered if the end product is to be used by small children, people who smoke, or for sleeping arrangements near hot registers or fireplaces. Also consider that synthetics do not breathe. For some, a polyester quilt is like covering up with a sheet of plastic, causing the skin to perspire and body heat to build up. For others, the added warmth is needed.

In short, buyer beware. Manufacturers are researching and developing new products that will eliminate as many of the hazards as possible. However, we as consumers need to use personal judgement. Test all materials to be sure that they will perform the way you expect.

Use the following chart as a reference for your future batting needs. Information as to yardage requirements for batting is discussed in Chapter 8.

Batting Chart

Brand Name	Fiber Content	Quilting Distance	Appearance	Characteristics	Uses	Sizes Available
Mountain Mist 100% Natural Cotton	100% cotton	1/4" – 1"	Antique appearance. Puckers from shrinkage.	5%+ shrinkage. Not bonded. Layers stick together. Cool in summer; warm in winter. Adjusts to body temperature. Drapable, cuddly. Breathes.	Antique quilt tops, antique quilt reproductions, wall quilts, baby quilts, hot pads.	81" x 96" 81" x 108"
Mountain Mist Blue Ribbon	100% cotton	1½" – 2"	Flat, thin, antique appearance.	Moderate to no shrinkage. Bonded. Layers stick together. Breathes. Cool in summer. Adjusts to body temperature.	Antique quilt tops, antique quilt reproductions, wall quilts, baby quilts, hot pads, clothing.	90" x 108"
Fairfield Cotton Classic	80% cotton 20% polyester	2" – 3"	Flat, thin.	Moderate to no shrinkage. Shrinkage allowance should be checked. (refer to page 28). Can be presoaked if desired. Breathes. Cool in summer.	Quilts, wall quilts, baby quilts, tablecloths, placemats, clothing.	36" x 45" 81" x 96"
P & B or First Run Fabrics Double Brushed Cotton Flannelette	100% cotton High quality with adequate thread count.	Variable	Flat, very thin. Can shrink to give antique appearance.	No loft. Light weight.	Baby quilts, lap robes, summer-weight coverlets, tablecloths, placemats, clothing.	36" and 45" wide by the yard
Taos Mountain Wool Works Traditional™ and Designer Light™	100% wool	1" – 4"	Resilient, thin to moderate loft.	Warm in cold, damp climates. Cool in warm weather compared to polyester. Resists soiling. Needle-punched. Recommended to be encased in cheesecloth.	Quilts, lap robes, clothing.	90" wide by the yard 60" x 90" 80" x 90" 90" x 90" 90" x 108"
Generic Wool (from numerous sources)	100% wool	1" – 4"	Puffy, resilient.	Must be encased in cheesecloth. High resilience. Warm in cold, damp climates.	Tied comforters and quilts.	Varies
Mountain Mist Glazene Process 100% Polyester and Mountain Mist Quilt-Light	100% polyester	1/8" – 2½"	Thin to moderately puffy.	Fibers shift to fill space available. Can be quilted extremely close without getting stiff. Does not shrink. Look and feel of cotton. Heat sensitive.	Bed quilts, lap quilts.	45" x 60" 72" x 90" 81" x 96" 90" x 108" 120" x 120"
Fairfield Low Loft, Extra Loft, Hi Loft and Hobbs Poly-Down, Poly-Down-DK	100% polyester	2" – 4"	Moderate to high loft. Various lofts range from 1/4" – 3" thick.	Warm, lightweight, heat sensitive. Stretches and distorts if hung. Low recovery from compression. Does not shrink.	Bed quilts, lap quilts, pillows	45" x 60" 72" x 90" 81" x 96" 90" x 108" 120" x 120"

Techniques

Quilt-as-You-Go Techniques

AS YOU BEGIN TO DISCOVER the excitement and fun of machine quilting, you will want to start with small projects and work up to larger ones. Depending on the batting chosen and the size of the quilt, you may prefer to quilt in sections as opposed to quilting one large, bulky piece. This gives you more maneuverability than when working with a large quilt that is all in one piece. This chapter will teach you how to quilt as you go so that you can choose which method is best for you.

Before assembling the quilt blocks to make your quilt top, make a graph of the quilt top on paper to determine section divisions. Use the following to figure the available width of the lining fabrics when planning your quilt: Lining fabric is likely to be 45 inches wide. Once you subtract 1 inch for selvages and 1 inch for seam allowances, approximately 42 inches of usable width remains to accommodate the quilt sections. Base your section sizes on a 42-inch-wide piece of fabric.

Let's work through an example. You are making a quilt, with no borders, which measures 80 inches by 90 inches finished. You are using a 10-inch block. The blocks are set together 8 blocks wide and 9 blocks long. The 80 inches can be divided evenly by two to obtain two 40-inch sections across the width of the quilt. The lining (42 inches) will accommodate this. The 90-inch length can be divided into 3 sections, each 30 inches long. This will give you a section that is easy to handle.

The quilt top shown in Figure 7.1 is 80 inches by 90 inches. The top is divided evenly into six sections, each four blocks wide by three blocks long. Each unit measures 40 inches by 30 inches keeping within the lining width.

Before setting the blocks together, lay them out in order on the floor to make sure the pattern repeat is correct. Then sew them together into the section sizes determined. It may be necessary for you to label or number the sections to keep them in their proper order as you work.

Once the sections are constructed, determine the size needed for the batting and lining. These need to be at least 2 inches larger than each quilt section

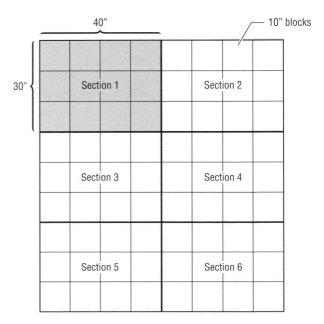

FIG. 7.1 Dividing quilt into sections

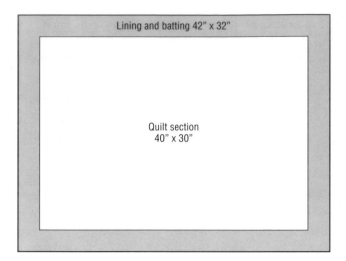

FIG. 7.2 Layered quilt section

on all four sides to allow for contraction while quilting, as well as extra ease when joining the seams.

Lining and batting for this example would need to be cut 42 inches by 32 inches (Figure 7.2).

Your quilt top will not always divide into an even number of blocks in each section. Figure 3.3 shows a quilt top that finishes 77 inches by 84 inches. If the blocks are 7 inches square, they are placed 11 across the width of the quilt and 12 down the length. When you draw a graph on paper of your quilt, put 5 blocks across in one section and 6 blocks across the other section. The length can be divided evenly into 3 sections. This gives you 3 sections that are 6 blocks across and 4 blocks long (42 inches by 28 inches) and 3 sections that are 5 blocks across and 4 blocks long (35 inches by 28 inches). Now fig-

ure the size of the batting and lining by adding 2 inches for contraction and joining seams.

This example demonstrates possible problems with lining sizes. You can see that one section is 42 inches wide. When placed with a 42-inch piece of lining, there is no allowance for contraction. You need to run the lengthwise grain of the fabric across the width of the quilt. The lining width of 42 inches will easily accommodate the 28-inch length of each section. An alternative to this is to divide the quilt into more sections, accommodating the lining by keeping the width of each section less than 40 inches wide.

Or, the top section can be constructed so that you have long strips the full length of the quilt. This requires less finishing on the back since there are fewer pieces. Depending on your level of comfort with machine quilting, this option should be considered.

An alternate method of dividing the quilt into sections, if the design allows, is to split the center block itself (Figure 7.4). Even patch designs (i.e., 2, 4, 6 patch blocks, etc.) are excellent for this method. A 77-by-84-inch quilt, containing even patch blocks, is easily split into 6 equal-sized sections. Figure 7.4 shows each section containing 5 full blocks, and ½ of the center block. This division also allows the lining seam to be centered on the back of the quilt.

NOTE: If you are adding borders to your quilt, they must be considered when drawing diagrams for figuring lining and batting sizes. Add their width

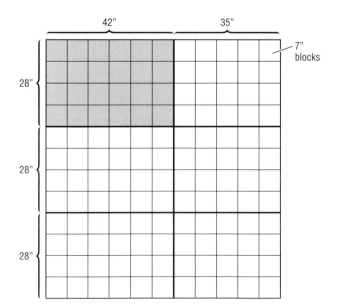

FIG. 7.3 Sectioned quilt top

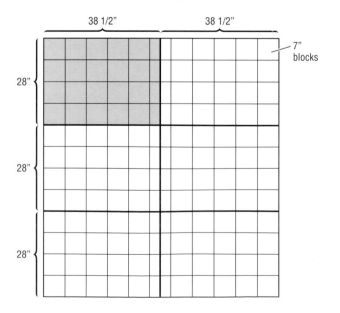

FIG. 7.4 Splitting center quilt block

to the quilt sections when figuring section size. Borders are added after the quilt sections are quilted and joined, but batting and lining allowances must be made before the quilting process. When all sections are joined, there is a margin of batting and lining left to accommodate the border piece. Refer to Figure 7.12.

LAYERING QUILT-AS-YOU-GO SECTIONS

Work smaller units on a tabletop or counter when layering. Use masking or drafting tape to tape the lining down to the surface. Stretch it, keeping it tight and free from sagging and shifting. Place the batting on top of the lining, keeping the edges even. Lining and batting should always be the same size. Be sure to place the quilt top sections onto the batting and lining evenly, leaving slightly less allowance around the edges which are joined to another section.

After placing the quilt top section on the batting, label each section to identify its position within the quilt. Check that the patchwork pattern meets correctly with the adjoining section. To avoid a section mix-up, lay the sections out on the floor. Double-check that each section is in the proper place before quilting.

Refer to Chapter 9 for layering techniques. If you have layered and pinned the quilt sections properly, the quilting will be trouble-free. Improper or insufficient layering techniques can lead to lumping and puckering of both the back and the front of the quilt.

After the sections are layered, they are ready to be quilted. Read and practice the techniques given in Chapters 11, 12, and 13 to determine what type of quilting is appropriate for your quilt.

NOTE: When quilting a quilt-as-you-go section, be sure to begin your stitching on the section edges which will eventually be joined to another section. Begin the stitching at least 1 inch in from these edges. This allows any excess fullness that might be present to be eased to the outer edges. It also allows for a margin of unstitched area, enabling you to seam the sections together. The quilting lines will be connected later, once the sections are joined.

QUILT-AS-YOU-GO COMES TOGETHER

After quilting the sections, join them into one large piece before adding borders and binding.

Lay the quilt sections out on the floor to check proper position. Join the sections vertically first, creating rows the length of the quilt. You will be sewing horizontal seams. Lay the two sections to be joined on a flat surface with the lining side up. Pin back the lining and batting, exposing the wrong side of the quilt top. With right sides together, stitch the two sections, matching all seams, points and corners. Sew a ¼-inch seam, or sew the same measurement used in the piecing of the blocks (Figure 7.5).

FIG. 7.5 Blocks sewn together

On the right side of the quilt, lightly press the seam allowance to one side using a warm iron. Press all seams in that row the same direction. Alternate the pressing direction from one row to another. Continue this process until all sections are joined in their respective rows (Figure 7.6).

Lay all the sections on a flat surface with the lining side up. Unpin the batting and lining. Smooth

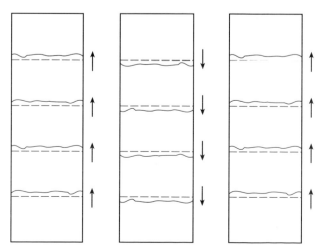

FIG. 7.6 Joining blocks for each row

the batting, laying one side on top of the other. Cut through the two layers of batting so that the two pieces butt together (see Figure 7.7). Using a herringbone stitch (Figures 7.8 and 7.9), connect the batting edges together to prevent shifting. Repeat for all seams in each row.

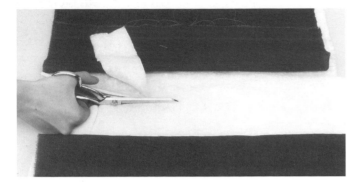

FIG. 7.7   Trimming the batting

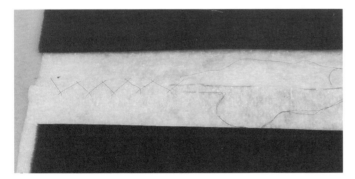

FIG. 7.8   Joining the batting

FIG. 7.9   Herringbone stitch illustration

When the batting is secured, finish the lining seams by using the following method: Turn the sections over so that the quilt top faces up. Place pins every 1½ inches in the seam that joins the sections. The pins should be pushed to the back so that their points stand upright when the sections are turned over. Now turn the sections over again so that the lining faces up. Fold the lining back on each side so that the fold rests against the pin markers. Pin each folded edge in place. Remove pin markers. Press the folded edges, then remove the remaining pins. Repeat this method for each section (Figure 7.10).

Unfold the pressed lining edge. Trim excess lining to within ½ inch from crease (Figure 7.10). Lay the lining of section 1 out flat. Smooth any ripples between the quilting and the edge. Fold the lining

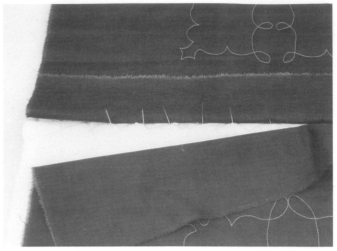

FIG. 7.10   Pin marking for lining seam placement

edge of section 2 under along the creased line (Figure 7.11). Match the fold of section 2 to the creased line of section 1. Beginning in the center of the line, pin baste every inch through all layers, stopping 2 inches from the end of the lining. Lift the 2-inch section of the lining away from the batting and pin. This area needs to be left free to accommodate joining one row to another. Blindstitch with ⅛-inch stitches, using a single thread the same color as the lining. NOTE: Be sure the 2 inches on the ends are kept free of the batting while blindstitching. Also make sure that your blind stitches do not show through to the quilt top. Repeat this for the remaining seams in each row. The folded lining closures should all be lapped in the same direction.

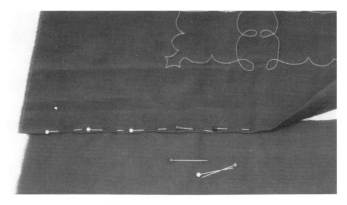

FIG. 7.11   Blindstitching seam

On the quilt top, connect any quilting lines over the seams just made by connecting the sections. Now you are ready to join the rows. Stitch row 1 to row 2, matching all seams, points and corners. Press seam to one side. Repeat the same techniques for trimming the batting and folding the lining as you did to join the sections.

After the long seams are finished, add the borders. Measure the length of the quilt through the center of the quilt. Measure the border fabric to be the same length and sew the lengthwise borders onto each side. The border can be sewn through all three layers (top, batting and lining) or added to the quilt top section only. When the border is opened and smoothed over the batting, there is sufficient batting and lining to accommodate it (Figure 7.12).

Quilt-as-you-go is only one method to prepare your quilt top for machine quilting. It does offer the beginner more manuverability and ease of bulk than doing the whole quilt at once. This method also allows you to work with thick, bulky battings in large quilts. As your skills increase, you will find that it is preferable to do many of your quilts as whole quilts.

FIG. 7.12 Attaching border

The whole-quilt methods are explained in Chapters 8, 9 and 10.

WEDDING DRESS

machine quilted by the author

free-motion and stippling techniques

quilting time: 9 hours

Cotton Classic batting

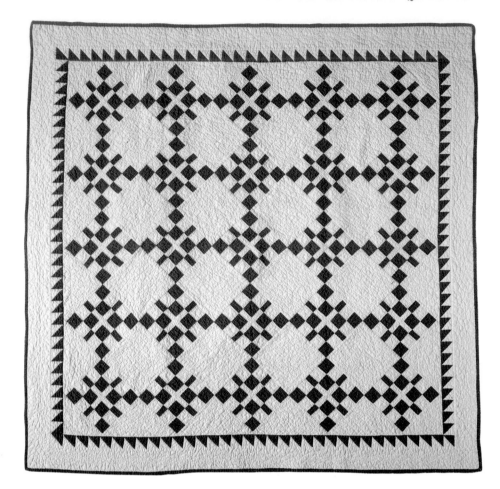

STAR CHAIN
68" x 68"
Harriet Hargrave
machine pieced and quilted
continuous curve and free-motion
techniques
100% Natural cotton batting

OHIO ROSE
62" x 62"
Harriet Hargrave
machine appliqued and quilted
echo and grid quilting techniques
100% Natural cotton batting

SCRAP NINE-PATCH

60" x 72"

Harriet Hargrave

reproduction of quilt by

Jean Wilbur,

Columbia Cross Roads, PA

machine pieced and quilted

free-motion techniques

100% Natural cotton batting

LANCASTER ROSE

45" x 45"

Harriet Hargrave

machine appliqued and quilted

free-motion techniques

Mountain Mist Glazene polyester batting

**CENTENNIAL STAR
AUTOGRAPH QUILT**

53" x 62"

Harriet Hargrave

machine pieced and quilted

continuous curve techniques

Blue Ribbon batting

LONE STAR

(corner detail)

80" x 90"

Sandy Espenschied, Atlanta, GA

free-motion, continuous curve and

straight-line techniques

Blue Ribbon batting

BOSTON COMMONS VARIATION

70" x 70"

Sandy Espenschied,

Atlanta, GA

machine pieced

and quilted

grid, stippling, and

free-motion techniques

Blue Ribbon batting

BOSTON COMMONS BACK

(detail of feathers, stippling, and grid work)

AMISH SHADOWS

39" x 52"

Harriet Hargrave

machine pieced and quilted

ditch and free-motion techniques

Cotton Classic batting

AMISH STRAWS

38" x 38"

Sandy Espenschied, Atlanta, GA

free-motion and straight-line quilting

Blue Ribbon batting

SMELL THE SPRING FLOWERS

54" x 54"

Betty Gilliam, Stillwater, OK

machine pieced and quilted

continuous curve, stippling, and

free-motion techniques

Mountain Mist Quilt-Light batting

FEATHERED RADIANT STAR

25" x 25"

Mary Lambert, Washington, IL

machine pieced and quilted

free-motion and stippling techniques

100% Natural cotton batting

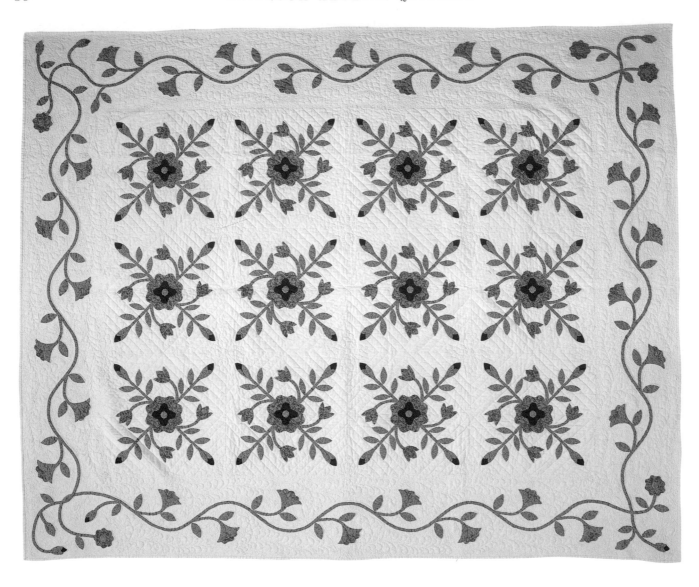

ROSE OF SHARON

76" x 93"

Sue Rasmussen, Simi Valley, CA

machine appliqued and quilted

25 hours

100% Natural cotton batting

ROSE OF SHARON

(detail of quilting in the corner)

A WINTERS SLEIGH RIDE

39" x 49"

Sue Rasmussen, Simi Valley, CA

Original pattern by Jean Johnson

hand appliqued and machine quilted

free-motion, stippling, and grid quilting techniques

Mountain Mist Glazene polyester batting

A WINTERS SLEIGH RIDE

(detail of stippling in ice)

WINTER STARS

85" x 100"

Betty Gilliam, Stillwater, OK

Colors inspired by winter ice storm

machine pieced and quilted

free-motion and ditch quilting techniques

Mountain Mist Quilt-Light batting

WINTER STARS

(detail of quilting on the back)

CARD TRICK

90" x 90"

Sandy Lawrence, Phoenix, AZ

machine pieced and quilted

stippling and straight-line techniques

100% Natural cotton batting

Sandy's first machine quilted quilt

POPPY SPRAY

(detail of quilting in corner)

68" x 84"

Deborah Ward, Arroyo Grande, CA

machine appliqued and quilted

free-motion and grid techniques

polyester bonded batting

TRIPLE IRISH CHAIN

84" x 104"

Sandy Lawrence, Phoenix, AZ

machine pieced and quilted

free-motion, grid, and stipple techniques

needlepunched polyester batting

MACHINE QUILTED SAMPLER

24" x 24"

Harriet Hargrave

machine pieced, appliqued, and quilted using

various techniques

needlepunched polyester batting

DOUBLE NINE-PATCH

50" x 60"

Mary Lambert, Washington, IL

machine pieced and quilted

free-motion and stipple techniques

100% Natural cotton batting

MONTANA SKIES

52" x 52"

Marla Yeager, Overland Park, KS

machine pieced and quilted

free-motion and stippling techniques

100% Natural cotton batting

**BLUE VALLEY NORTH
SPIRIT SHIRT**

Marla Yeager, Overland Park, KS

machine embroidery

and stipple quilting

ANTIQUE QUILTED PETTICOAT

(detail of quilting in lower half of petticoat)

**ANTIQUE QUILTED
PETTICOAT AND BIB**

owned by Harriet Hargrave

early 1900's quilted garments

totally made by machine;

petticoat a gift to author

from Joe Buckley

both items found in Pennsylvania

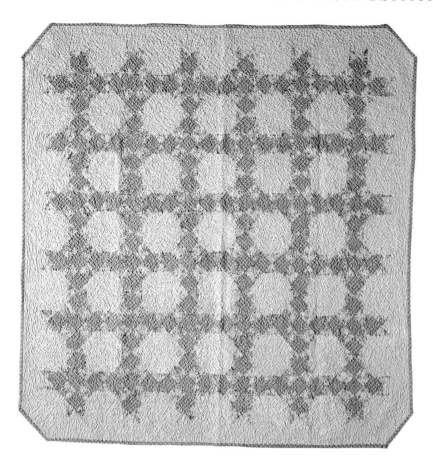

NINE-PATCH AND SNOWBALL
(tablecover)
60″ x 60″
Jean Lohmar, Galesburg, IL
totally machine stippled
Cotton Classic batting.

1920's WHIG ROSE
owned by
Harriet Hargrave
two lengths of fabric
machine quilted in ½″
grid, then joined
quilt-as-you-go method;
roses were hand
appliqued on top of
quilted fabric; binding
applied by machine in
ditch as described on
Chapter 14, page 98

BLUE MEDALLION

68" x 84"

Harriet Hargrave

machine pieced and quilted

continuous curve, free-motion, and echo techniques

Mountain Mist Glazene polyester batting

Lining For Whole Quilts

MACHINE QUILTING A LARGE QUILT top requires special handling, but it can be done easily following the methods presented in this unit. As with quilt-as-you-go, the whole-quilt method eliminates the need to join sections together and add borders after the quilting is completed.

Lining should be of the same fiber content as the top of the quilt. If you have used polyester blends in the piecing, the lining should also be a blend. If your top is 100% cotton, use only 100% cotton for the back or lining. If you have prewashed your fabrics before piecing your top, be sure to prewash your lining. Allow for 3% shrinkage in lining when figuring yardage. If you have not prewashed your fabric, do not prewash your lining.

Consider whether to use prints or solids. Muslin and bleached cotton, as well as solid colors, are traditional lining fabrics which really show off your quilting. If you are new to machine quilting, you may want to use a print. Small mistakes and uneven stitches are not as conspicuous on a print as they are on solids.

If you have light solids in the quilt top, dark linings can change the appearance of the top fabric, especially when using polyester battings. An example is using white in the quilt top, and a navy blue lining. If you use a polyester batt, the blue lining will cause the white fabric in the top to appear gray. Use cotton batting to eliminate this effect.

FIGURING YARDAGE FOR LININGS AND BATTINGS

When figuring yardage for the lining, allow for contraction. This is the width and length of the fabric used by the loft (thickness) of the batting, as well as by the stitching during the quilting process.

If you use a polyester batting ½ inch thick or more, you will need to allow 3 to 4 inches extra batting and lining per side than the size of the quilt top. Cotton, cotton blend, and thin polyester battings need to be 1½ to 2 inches larger on all sides than the quilt top. This excess is needed when machine quilting because the feed dogs tend to take in the lining fabric, and the presser foot flattens out the top, making the top layer larger. The thickness of the batting determines how much fabric is used in the loft, or puff, between the quilting lines. The thicker the batting, the more fabric required to accommodate the loft. A common complaint of machine quilting is that by the time you get to the edge of the quilt, you have 2 inches more quilt top than lining. This method of figuring yardage helps eliminate this problem.

Generally, 45-inch-wide yard goods are used for lining. Sheeting in 90-inch and 108-inch widths is also available in white and natural and more recently, in limited colors. Bed sheets are also used. These wider fabrics eliminate the need for seams in the lining. Be mindful of thread count and fiber content when shopping for sheets and wide sheeting fabrics for your linings.

Seaming is necessary when using 45-inch-wide fabric. Remember, it has a usable finished width of 40 to 42 inches. You cannot back an 87-inch-wide quilt top with just two widths of 45-inch fabric. You will have to subtract at least 1 inch for selvages and another 1 inch for seam allowances per width.

Sketch your quilt on paper to keep your figures accurate. Always allow for contraction. If you machine quilt an item and cut the lining and batting the same size as the quilt and then quilt it, the top piece will always push off the edge before you are finished. This shift is caused by the pressure of the presser foot pushing the top fabric, and by not allowing for the amount of fabric it takes to "puff up" between the quilting lines. By allowing 2 to 4 inches extra backing and batting on all sides of the quilt top,

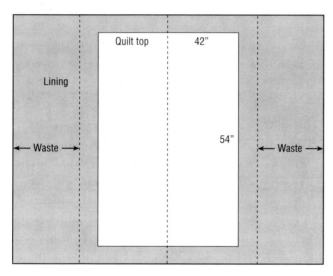

FIG. 8.1 Vertical lining seam

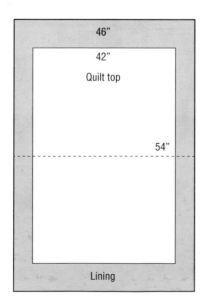

FIG. 8.2 Horizontal lining seam

you will eliminate the problems of fabric shortage and shifting.

To make the lining wide enough, at least one seam will be needed. Usually the seams run vertically with the quilt, but they may run either vertically or horizontally, whichever makes the most efficient use of the fabric. If more than one seam is required, try to balance the location of the panels so that the lining sections are balanced. Join the lengths together using a ½-inch seam. Cut away the selvages and sew ½ inch from the edge, or sew ¾ inch with the selvages left on. Clip through the selvage every 1 inch to prevent puckering along the seam. Press the seam allowances open.

Let's work through some examples. NOTE: All examples assume you are using ¼-inch-thick batting, which requires 2 inches allowance on all sides for contraction.

SMALL QUILTS

The most economical way to finish a small quilt is to keep it under 42 inches. However, if the quilt is wider than 42 inches, the lining needs to be seamed. Use simple math to see how to use the fabric efficiently:

Vertical seam method: The quilt is 42 inches by 54 inches. After adding for contraction, the lining should measure 46 inches by 58 inches, allowing for 2 inches on all sides. This requires two lengths of fabric, each 58 inches long. This is a total of 3¼ yards. Notice the waste from the excess width (Figure 8.1).

Horizontal seam method: If we run the seam horizontally, we need two lengths of lining 46 inches long, or 2⅔ yards. This is a more efficient use of the width of the fabric, as well as requiring less yardage (Figure 8.2).

TWIN- AND DOUBLE-SIZE QUILTS

Standard-size twin and double bed quilts need two lengths of lining fabric to accommodate their width. Some queen-size quilts can also follow these guides. Be sure to check your measurements.

If the quilt is 74 inches by 85 inches, you need two lengths of 45-inch-wide lining fabric. Adding 4 inches for contraction, you get 89 inches. Divide 89 inches by 36 inches (1 yard), which is 2½ yards each (Figure 8.3). You will need 2 lengths, 2½ yards each, for a total of 5 yards. Add 3% for shrinkage if you plan to prewash the fabric.

Let's practice figuring for horizontal seams (Figure 8.4). It takes 3 widths to cover the 89 inches of length for the quilt. There's a lot of waste from the

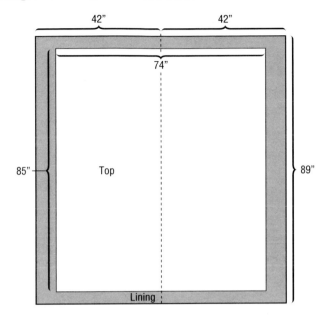

FIG. 8.3 Utilizing lining with vertical seam

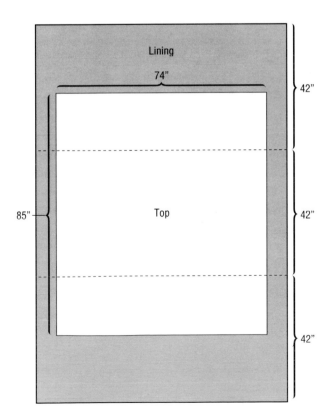

FIG. 8.4 Utilizing lining with horizontal seam

width of the lining: 3 by 42 inches = 126 inches when we only need 89 inches. Each length would be 2⅙ yards long (78 inches by 36 inches = 2⅙ yards) times the 3 lengths needed. This equals 6½ yards. This would not be an efficient use of fabric.

QUEEN- AND KING-SIZE QUILTS

The seam that joins the lining pieces can be centered down the middle in a twin or double lining. However, the larger-size quilts need 2½ to 3 widths of fabric. These seams should be evenly spaced, having one complete width down the center and balancing the remainder evenly on both sides.

If the quilt is 88 inches by 94 inches, the lining should be 92 inches by 98 inches to allow for contraction. Use one-width of fabric down the center. Figure this as 42 inches wide after seams and selvages are subtracted. Since the lining needs to be 92 inches wide, subtract 42 inches from 92 inches: You will need 50 inches of width. If this width is divided by 2, you find you need 25 inches more on each side of the center piece (Figure 8.5).

We now know we need 3 lengths of fabric to accommodate the width of the quilt. Each length should be 2¾ yards (98 inches by 36 inches). 2¾ yards by 3 lengths is 8¼ yards for the lining (Figure 8.6).

Try figuring this same quilt using horizontal seams. You should find only ⅜-yard difference. In this case, preference for vertical or horizontal seams is the deciding factor as to which method to use (Figure 8.7).

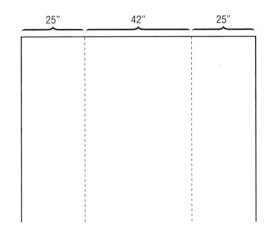

FIG. 8.5 Lining construction

One last example for a king-size quilt: The quilt measures 100 inches by 120 inches. The lining needs to be 104 inches by 124 inches. To figure for vertical seams, divide the width of the quilt by 42 inches to see how many lengths of fabric are needed. This is 104 by 42 = 3 lengths. The quilt length plus contraction allowances is divided by 36 inches: 124 inches by 36 inches = 3½ yards. 3 lengths times 3½ yards is 10½ yards (Figure 8.8).

To figure for horizontal seams, divide the length by 42 inches: 124 inches by 42 inches = 3 widths needed. Each length should be 104 inches long, or 104 inches by 36 inches = 3 yards. 3 yards times 3 lengths is 9 yards. By using horizontal seams instead of vertical ones, you can save 1½ yards of fabric (Figure 8.9).

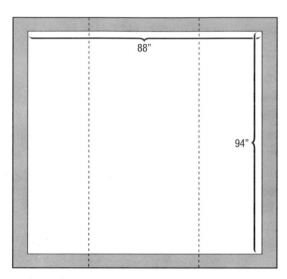

FIG. 8.6 Vertical seam

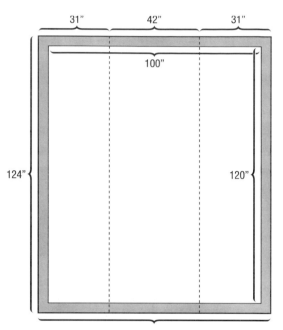

FIG. 8.8 Vertical seams

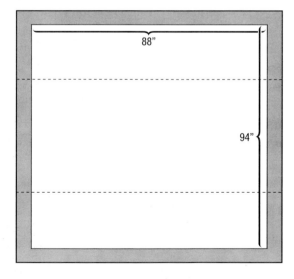

FIG. 8.7 Horizontal seam

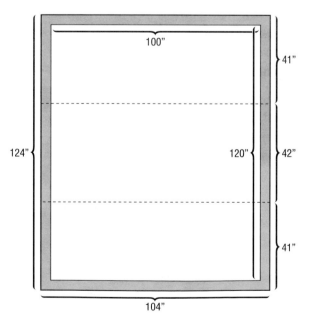

FIG. 8.9 Horizontal seams

Layering

ONCE THE QUILT BATTING HAS BEEN CHOSEN, the top has been squared and pressed well, and the quilting designs have been carefully marked onto the quilt top, you are ready to put the layers together and pin baste. Do not bind the quilt before quilting. If you have ever stretched and basted a quilt on the floor by the old, traditional methods, you are going to appreciate the method presented here. No more aching backs and sore knees!

Create a work surface that is about 3 feet wide and 5 feet to 6 feet long. This could be a sheet of plywood, a counter top, the dining room table, etc. Avoid using Ping-Pong and pool tables, as they are too wide and the lining fabric will not be stretched properly. To lessen back strain, raise the height of the table by placing stacks of books under the legs to achieve a comfortable height (usually at waist height). If you do not have a table to work on, cut a piece of ¾ inch plywood 3 feet by 6 feet, varnish it,

and place it on two sawhorses that you have made to be your working height. This is an inexpensive way to get a good working surface, and it can be taken down and put out of the way when not needed.

Measure the length and width of the table to find the center points on all four sides. Mark these centers with drafting tape. A student once suggested placing the tape over a toothpick so you can feel the bump through the layers of fabric throughout the process. Excellent idea!

Once the lining is sewn together and pressed well to remove all creases, fold in half lengthwise, wrong sides together. Also note the crosswise center of the lining. Place the folds on the tape guidelines, and unfold to one thickness, wrong side facing up. Allow the excess to hang over the edges of the table. The center of the lining should run down the center of the table.

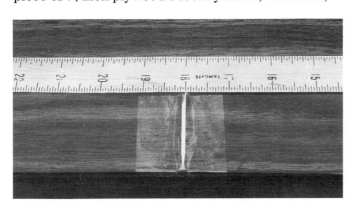

FIG. 9.1 Marking centers of table

FIG. 9.2 Centered lining

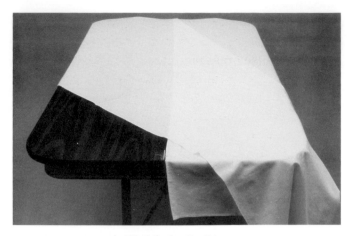

FIG. 9.3 Opening lining

Smooth the fabric over the table top. Using binder clips or any strong clamp that will fit your surface, stretch the lining over the table top: Begin by clamping one end using two or three clamps. Then stretch and clamp the opposite end. After clamping both ends, stretch and clamp the sides. Try to keep the lining as centered as possible. Use as many clamps as necessary to keep the lining smooth and taut, but do not stretch it so tightly that it could damage the fabric. You should be able to run your hand over the fabric and see no motion or crawling.

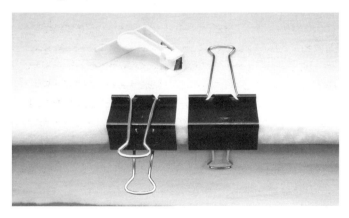

FIG. 9.4 Clamps for stretching

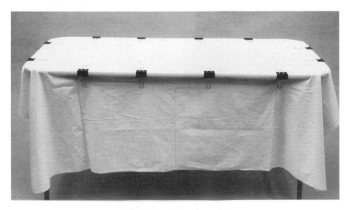

FIG. 9.5 Stretched lining

Stretching controls any fullness in the lining fabric before going to the machine so the feed dogs will not make any tucks and puckers. This virtually eliminates all distortion and tucks on the lining side.

NOTE: If the quilt or project is too small to clamp on one or more sides, use masking or drafting tape to tape the edges when stretching. This is sufficient for blocks, small wall quilts and baby quilts.

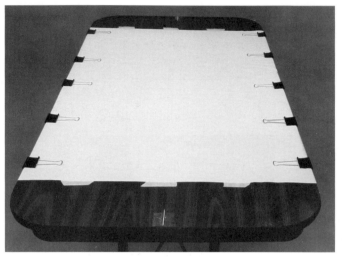

FIG. 9.6 Tape stretching

Next, fold the batting in half lengthwise. Make sure it is smooth and free of fold lines and stretch marks. If polyester batting is distorted from packaging, place it in the clothes dryer with a damp hand towel and tumble it, using the permanent press setting for 10 to 15 minutes. This should soften and remove the fold lines. The natural fiber batts will smooth out as you work with them.

Lay the fold at the center placement guides on top of the lining. Unfold the batting so that it hangs over the edges of the table. Smooth it out gently without stretching it. The lining and batting should

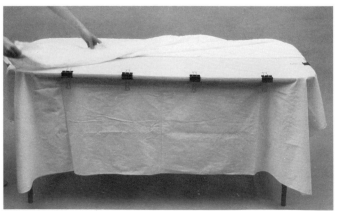

FIG. 9.7 Positioning batting

be the same size, and should be 2 to 4 inches larger than the quilt top.

Now you are ready for the quilt top. Fold the quilt top in half lengthwise, right sides together. Center the fold over the center placement guides (toothpicks), and open it so that it hangs over the edges of the table. The three layers should now be centered and stacked: lining, batting and quilt top.

Be careful not to stretch the quilt top; just smooth it gently over the batting. If the top was well pieced and properly pressed, it will smooth evenly. If not, there might be extra fullness in some places, tightness in others. Do not force these areas to lie flat, since that will cause distortion in other areas, especially the borders. You will need to work the fullness in as you quilt that area.

FIG. 9.8 Centering quilt top

FIG. 9.9 Layering completed

SAFETY PINS

You will need an abundant supply of #1, nickel-plated safety pins to pin baste the layers together. These pins are 1 inch long and have a fine tip that will leave a very small hole in the cloth. Large pins are easier to close, but they put damaging holes in the fabrics. Safety pins are used because they stay

in the quilt as it is rolled and re-rolled throughout the quilting process. Nickel-plated pins are preferred because brass pins can rust, and they may leave a black mark in the fabric where they are inserted. If you can find them in bulk, #0 pins are a little smaller and finer. At least 350 safety pins are needed to layer a double-size quilt, 500 or more for a king. Do not skimp on the number of pins that you use.

Regular basting will not hold up to machine quilting. It allows the layers to shift and bunch when packaging and re-rolling. Also, it tends to get caught in the foot as you sew, and it's difficult to remove after stitching over the threads with many rows of machine stitching. REMEMBER: The pinning and layering process is 90% of the success of machine quilting. If you have not layered well, you will have endless trouble as you attempt to quilt on the machine.

On thin, cotton-type batting, place the pins 3 to 4 inches apart. If a thicker, more wiry polyester-type batting is used, place the pins much closer together, approximately 2 to 3 inches apart. The more you can control the layers from shifting during the layering process, the easier the quilting will be.

When pinning the layers together, start in the center and work toward the corners. Try to avoid pinning across seam lines that will be ditch stitched or across any design lines. Place pins so that you can maneuver around them. Again, do not stretch and force any fabric to lie flat if it doesn't do so naturally. Ease the fullness in as you pin.

Once the table top area has been pinned, remove the clamps from all sides of the table. Slide the quilt layers to one side, so that the pins are hanging off

FIG. 9.10 Safety pin basting

one side of the table. On the opposite side of the table, reach under to find the lining. Gently stretch the lining only, using the pinned area to stretch against. Reclamp the lining onto the edge opposite from the pinned area. Then stretch the ends and reclamp them. Do not clamp the pinned side. The

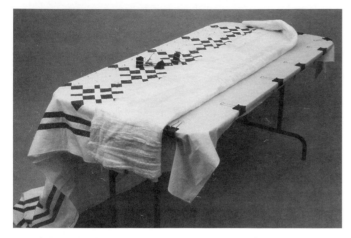

FIG. 9.11 Restretching lining after repositioning

weight from the pins will give enough resistance to keep the lining stretched. Reposition the batting and the quilt top, smooth, and start to pin the layers together from the pinned area to the opposite side. Repeat this process until that side is completely pinned. Repeat the process for the other side of the quilt, then again for the ends. You might want to rotate the quilt so that the ends are now placed on the length of the table to make it faster to stretch and pin baste.

Do not try to eliminate any of these steps. Once the entire quilt is pin basted, turn it over and run your hands over the surface. If any fullness backs up against a pin, you may need to unpin that area and restretch and repin to eliminate possible problems. This procedure also keeps your quilts from stretching and becoming distorted while machine quilting.

Packaging

WHETHER YOU ARE QUILTING a whole quilt or quilt-as-you-go sections, the following techniques apply. I have two general rules that I follow when preparing to quilt: First, never turn a quilt under the machine. Turning causes distortion from pushing the batting in too many directions. Besides this, it is very difficult, if not impossible, to successfully turn a large quilt and get all the excess through the 9-inch opening of your sewing machine. Second, have only half of the quilt under the machine at any time: Begin stitching on the center line, and once it is completed, move to the right. Continually unrolling the roll that is in the machine decreases it, making the quilting easier. Once that side is done, the quilt will be turned end-to-end and the process repeated for the other side. More detail on this will be given in the individual quilt section.

The first step in packaging is to lay the quilt right side up on a table. Work from the center line or row of blocks to the right. Fold the left side of the quilt up to the center line or row to within 2 inches from the line. The left side of the quilt will be supported by the table. Roll the right side of the quilt as tight as you can, also to within 2 inches from the center line. This is the side that goes through the machine and needs to be rolled tight so that it will fit. (Again, batting will make a difference in what size quilt you will be able to handle with this packaging process. You may need to quilt-as-you-go in sections.)

If the roll wants to come un-rolled, it will create problems when you try to manipulate the fabric to do the quilting lines. Bicycle pant-leg clips will hold the roll in place. These clips are made of spring steel and go around a large roll to secure it. Covering the clips with twill tape will keep them from sliding and scratching your machine. You will need four to 12 of these clips for large quilts. Place them down the length of the quilt, using enough to control the quilt. Use the clips on the left side if you find that it is trying to come unfolded. An added bonus to the clips is that the roll does not collapse as the length of the quilt extends behind the machine. When unrolling to the right for the next quilting line, you can unroll within the clips; they do not have to be removed each time. This speeds up the process immensely (See Figure 10.1).

Do a zigzag (accordion) fold from the end, making a compact package to put in your lap. It will automatically unfold as you work (See Figure 10.2).

Sit down at the machine with the package in your lap. Place the quilt under the machine at the

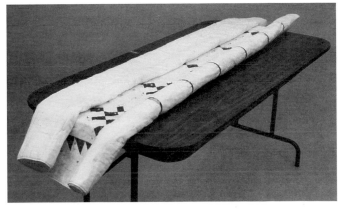

FIG. 10.1 Packaging process

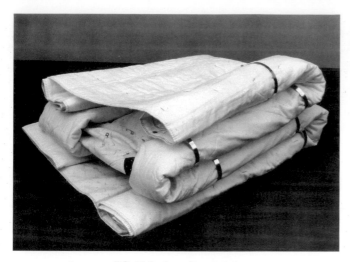

FIG. 10.2   Accordion pleated

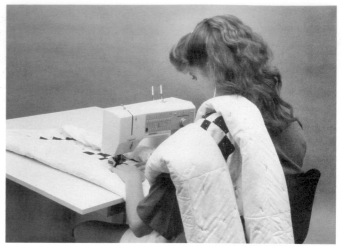

FIG. 10.4   Over shoulder position for diagonal set quilt

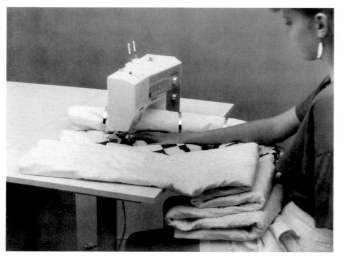

FIG. 10.3   Lap position for straight-set quilt

beginning of the line, and insert the needle. Adjust the quilt in your lap. Unroll or unfold a couple of times and "punch" it up under your chin so that the quilt is going down into the machine, not dragging up from your lap. Now you are ready to stitch.

If your quilting lines are diagonal in the quilt, use the same packaging technique, but roll the right side in from the corner point, and fold the left side from the opposite corner point. Instead of folding the length of the quilt into a square package, throw it over your left shoulder and feed it into the machine. (When folded diagonally, the quilt package tends to fall apart.) Use your shoulder and arm to keep the sides rolled, and feed into the machine consistently.

TIP: Do not wear a cotton or other natural fiber blouse or shirt when doing this, or the quilt will stick to you, making progress difficult. Instead, wear a slick polyester blouse that will shed the cotton fabrics.

This is the general packaging process. Each quilt will have a specific order in which things need to be done. Now you know all you need to start learning machine quilting techniques.

Straight-Line Quilting

THE EASIEST AND MOST COMMON form of machine quilting is quilting in the ditch. This is not a decorative technique, but many quilt patterns do not justify fancy quilting on the surface of the quilt. If the piecing design is very strong or if the fabric pattern is busy and predominant, the quilting generally won't show over it. Stitching in the ditch is a functional way to secure the three layers together. This method is also used to anchor between the blocks before doing surface quilting within the blocks. This makes the quilt much more stable and makes it easier to control under the machine's foot (Figure 11.1). Grid quilting, another common form of machine quilting, adds surface texture to strong designs without adding pattern. Unlike ditch quilting, grid quilting gives an overall quilted effect that can enhance many quilts.

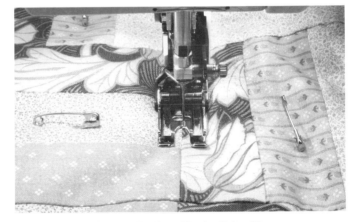

FIG. 11.1 Needle position for ditch quilting

DITCH QUILTING TECHNIQUES

The ditch method is good for beginning machine quilters. It is done with the walking foot to create long, straight lines. This foot does use a feeding system, so care must be taken to prevent shifting layers. Remember, do not turn the quilt under the machine, and only half of the bulk is under the machine at any time.

The ditch is created by pressing the seam allowance to one side, leaving a high side and a low side to the seam. When ditch quilting, the needle should always be on the low side, just rubbing the high side edge as you are stitching. When the seam is stitched and the fabric relaxes, the stitching is completely hidden in the fold. When you are constructing and pressing the patchwork, carefully press the seams so that no accordion pleats are formed.

Before starting any project, make it a habit to test your machine on a sample of the fabric and batting that will be used in the quilt. Once this sandwich is made, quilt a few rows of stitches, checking that the tension and stitch length are correct. You are looking for perfect, balanced tension that shows no loops of bobbin thread on the top surface, and no loops of top thread on the lining. Adjust your tensions accordingly (refer to page 5 for more information). The desirable stitch length is similar to the length you like in hand quilting. Remember, a stitch that is too short will perforate and weaken the fibers, and can cause tearing when stress is applied to the quilt. A stitch that is too long will break when stress is applied. A stitch about ⅛-inch long, or slightly shorter, is a durable length for machine quilting. When running sample stitches, check on the back to be sure that the stitches are consistently the same length. If they are erratic, your walking foot may not be mounted properly, or you are using your hands too much, not allowing the foot to do all the feeding.

When ditch or grid quilting a project, anchoring is easy to do, and allows the layers to remain straight and free of distortion. Stitch the anchor lines first when starting to quilt. They are the very center seamlines in the quilt, both lengthwise and crosswise. (If there is no seam in the very center of the quilt, move to the first seam to the right of the center.) You quilt these two lines first so that the quilt cannot shift and distort as you continue on quilting the other lines. If you fail to do this, the layers will tend to shift in the direction the foot is pushing, causing the border and corner to get out of square. This is a common problem for beginners. Read through all the instructions before beginning, and try the method first on the practice block or quilt. This will give you a chance to master the skills and techniques before moving on to a larger project.

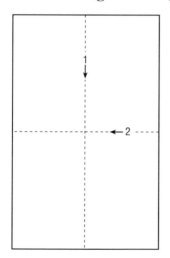

FIG. 11.2 Anchoring

Begin quilting on the center lengthwise seam. Position the block so that the very center lengthwise seam is exposed. Remember, when packaging a larger project, the left side is folded to within 2 inches of the seam and the right side is rolled as tight as you can get it and clamped with bicycle clips. Accordion pleat the quilt from the bottom up and place it under the machine. Review Chapter 10 for this information.

FIG. 11.3 Holding threads on edge

If you are on the raw edge of the block, hold both the top and bobbin threads tightly in your left hand as you begin to stitch.

If there is a border or sashing strip around the block, the stitching will begin inside the border at the border seamline.

FIG. 11.4 Holding threads inside border

Bring the bobbin thread to the surface before beginning to stitch by taking one complete stitch, either manually with the hand wheel or by using the automatic needle-up position on newer machines. Make sure that the needle is in its highest position when you stop. Move the fabric over slightly and pull on the top thread. The bobbin thread should appear up through the hole. Pull it through so that you can hold onto it as you begin the stitching. While holding the threads, insert the needle into the ditch, and lower the walking foot.

The thread tails need to be locked off before starting to quilt. Stitching in place and backstitching are not the best methods for locking the thread into the fabric. Instead, make a ¼-inch row of very tiny stitches buried in the ditch to keep the thread from creeping out. To do this, put your stitch length near "0" or about 24 to 30 stitches per inch. Stitch for ¼-inch distance at this setting. These stitches are so small that they cannot pull out. Once this is done, move the length regulator to the number that you found suitable on your sample, generally 2½ to 3, or 9 to 12 stitches per inch. When the stitching is locked off, clip the thread tails even with the surface of the fabric. This method keeps you from having to weave the threads back into the batting or tying them off. This locking system is critical when using nylon thread.

As you begin to stitch at the normal length stitch, do not help the machine more than is necessary by pushing, shoving and pulling the fabric through the foot. This will only lead to distortion and tucks. The walking foot is designed to feed the top layer of fabric evenly with the lining as it is pulled through the feed dogs. Train your hands to work with the fabric and the foot. Do not push and pull. REMEMBER: Keep your fingers in front of the foot, assisting it in easing any fullness in the top layer only.

You will often see that the top layer wants to push ahead a bit, and when you come to a seam, a small tuck will appear. This can be eliminated by feeding that excess fabric to the foot while stitching the length of the seam. To do this, place the fingers of one hand against the pins in the area, while the fingers of the other hand push any fullness — of the top only — toward the foot (Figure 11.5). Be careful that you do not also push the batting and lining. As you stitch, allow the walking foot to gently pull this

FIG. 11.5 Feeding fabric to walking foot

excess fabric into itself. As it does this, it will evenly ease out the fullness within the stitches. There should be no gathering, tucks or pleats. Gently walk your fingers just in front of the walking foot for the entire length of the seam. Use your fingers to position any extra fabric in front of the foot.

Stretching the seam in front of and behind the foot to prevent tucks from being sewn in will only distort the quilt when finished. When the batting is stretched and then stitched, it will try to rebound to its original shape, creating dips and valleys at the cross-seams, and fluting at the edges. If you follow the guidelines for feeding the excess fullness, the quilt will lie flat without tucks or distortion. Allow the walking foot to work for you, easing the fullness in gradually and consistently the full length of the seam.

If you are experiencing problems seeing, adjust the height of your chair. Retrain your eyes to watch the needle and know where it is going with every stitch. If you watch the foot and compensate for the position of the foot in relation to the seam, the needle will not be where it needs to be at any given time. If you watch the needle, you have the control to adjust the seam to accommodate the needle's position. Raising the height of your chair will eliminate glare from the machine light, and will allow you to see the hole where the needle is stitching. (Refer to page 4 for more information on chair height.)

As you approach the last ½ inch of the seam, slow down and start to decrease the stitch length. Be sure that the last ¼ inch of the seam is made up of very tiny stitches (24 to 30 stitches to the inch) to lock off the end of the stitching.

Now go back and examine the seam for quality and technique problems. The stitching should be on the low side of the ditch at all times. You do not want to see stitches on the fold of the high side. The stitches should be consistently the same length.

NOTE: Often the walking foot will hang up on bulky seam allowances. If this happens, you will see a few tiny stitches in that area. When you feel this happen with your foot, stop, lift the foot slightly, and set it down again. This will release the fabric that gets snagged under the foot. If this happens a lot, you can shave a bit of the plastic off of the center back feeder on the walking foot. This small piece of plastic can get stuck on the bulk of the seam allowances and "high center" the rest of the foot. By shaving some of it off, it does not catch as often.

There should be no gathers, tucks or stretched areas along the seam. Finally, the area where seams cross each other should be exactly perpendicular and square. If the line sags below a straight line, the fabric has been allowed to push ahead, and the quilt will look distorted when finished. If any of these things happen, go back and practice the feeding technique.

DITCH QUILTING EXERCISES

Practice these techniques on a block such as an Ohio Star that is pieced with many seams, or use a large square made of many small squares sewn together. A small quilt would also be suitable for this exercise. You will learn to stay in the ditch, and feed the fabric properly while using the walking foot. Follow the techniques previously given, and ditch quilt the center lengthwise seam from the top edge (or top border seam) through to the bottom edge (or bottom border seam). Handle the block as if it were a full-size quilt.

Next, quilt the center crosswise seamline. Refold and reroll so that the center crosswise seam is exposed. This is the second anchor seam. Stitch from the side edge (or border seam) to the opposite side edge (or border seam). If you are not feeding properly, a tuck will appear as you cross the first anchor line. Again, do not stretch the fabric to eliminate it. Remove the seam and try again. This time, ease the fullness up to the foot as you go. Finally, examine the seam for quality. This completes the anchoring seams which will help prevent the layers from shifting throughout the rest of the quilting process.

Once you have anchored the quilt, you are ready to continue with the remaining seams. Re-package the quilt again, this time lengthwise. You will continue to stitch the seams that are to the right of the center until you reach the border. Each stitching line will begin at the top border or edge and continue down through the anchor line to the bottom border or edge. Lock off the stitches at the beginning and end of every seam. Unroll the roll to the next line, fold up the left side more, and quilt the

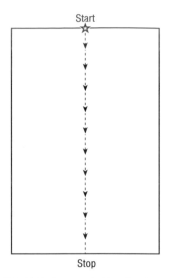

FIG. 11.6   Correct stitching direction

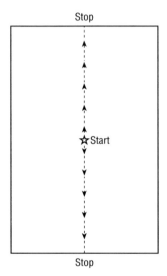

FIG. 11.7   Incorrect stitching direction

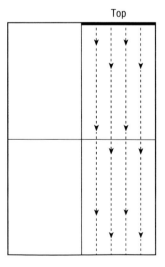

FIG. 11.8   Stitching each line right of center

next line to the right from the top border or edge to the bottom border or edge. Continue until the side is completed (Figure 11.8).

Re-package the quilt, but this time the roll will consist of the unquilted, lengthwise seams, and the fold on the left will be the previously quilted area. We have now turned the quilt end for end, so that the true bottom of the quilt is in the top position. Repeat the above instructions, working to the right, until all the lengthwise lines are stitched (Figure 11.9).

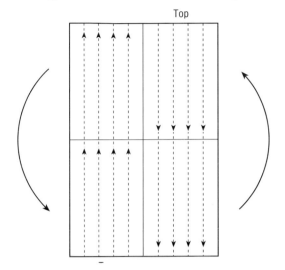

FIG. 11.9 Stitching opposite side

The crosswise seams are quilted next. The quilting becomes easier because the quilt is now well secured. You will now cross the lengthwise quilted seams. Continue to work with the walking foot to eliminate all tucks at the seam crossings. Re-package the quilt so that the crosswise seams are ready to be quilted. Quilt from the center out to the right, top to bottom, until all seams are quilted. Rotate the quilt so that the other side is now on your right (top) and repeat (Figure 11.10).

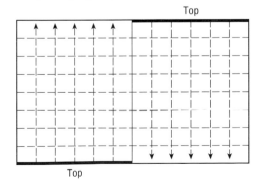

FIG. 11.10 Stitching cross seams

NOTE: I treat the seam that attaches the border onto the top as one of the seams to be quilted in the above order, instead of trying to quilt it in a square after all the rest of the quilt is quilted. (The borders are added to the top before the quilt is layered.)

This eliminates having to turn corners with the foot, which can push the batting slightly, causing the corner to stretch or cup up. Double-check your work to make sure you are keeping the quilt square and straight. After reviewing the section on free-motion quilting you will be ready to quilt the borders.

Once you are finished, check your project for quality. Look for adequate, small lock-off stitches at the beginning and end of each line of stitching. All seams should be straight and free of tucks and puckers. If there is distortion of the fabric between stitching lines, you need to improve your technique when working with the foot and the feeding system. Check the back of the quilt and make sure that all stitches are the same size (within reason) and that there are no tucks or gathering on the backing fabric. All of these small details need attention if you want to master machine quilting. Trim the edges, square the corners, and bind. You are now well on your way to finishing all those tops in the closet!

The Rail Fence quilt pictured below is just one example of a pattern that is perfect for a first ditch quilting project. Individual blocks are sewn together into rows, then the rows are sewn together. These joining seams make a perfect place to ditch quilt, giving the quilt a puffy texture and appearance, and stabilizing the layers. There is no need to add additional quilting to the surface if you have chosen your batting wisely.

Ditch quilting is often used alone, as with the Rail Fence quilt pictured below. It is more often used to secure the layers together before adding surface

FIG. 11.11 Rail Fence quilt

quilting designs using the free-motion techniques discussed in Chapter 13.

GRID QUILTING TECHNIQUES

FIG. 11.12 Diagonal grid quilting

Grid quilting is simply stitching straight or diagonal lines at equal intervals over the top of the pattern, regardless of design (Figure 11.12). It is a very functional type of quilting which adds a wonderful relief effect to the overall quilt. Grid quilting is often seen on antique quilts since it is a fast method of hand quilting. Strong and durable, it is a marvelous way to do extensive, close quilting on the machine for quilts such as Log Cabin, Pineapple and other old, traditional quilt patterns. The grids can either be

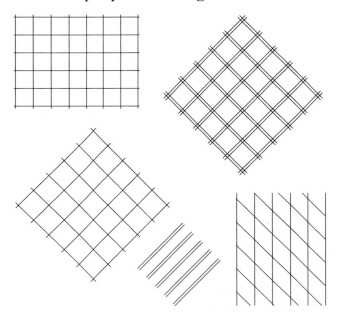

FIG. 11.13 Various grid patterns

straight, diagonal, double diagonal, hanging diamonds, or any combination you choose as illustrated in Figure 11.13. You will probably need to mark the lines on the quilt top to keep the lines straight and parallel. The rug canvas method described on page 19 is useful in helping you place the lines on the quilt top. Check Chapter 4 for other ways to mark parallel lines.

HANGING DIAMOND GRID

Pineapples and Log Cabins

FIG. 11.14 Pineapple with hanging diamond quilting

Some quilts are not enhanced by ditch quilting. Often a quilt needs straight-line quilting, but ditch quilting will not add surface texture. Log Cabins and many other quilts are so busy and complete in their design from the piecing or fabrics that fancy quilting is lost. An old, traditional way to achieve a heavy amount of quilting using straight lines, yet adding diagonal lines for interest, is called hanging diamonds. This technique uses straight lines, parallel to the border, for the lengthwise direction of the quilt, and one-directional diagonal lines (Figure 11.14 and 11.15).

When deciding which direction to quilt first, take into consideration the position of the lengthwise grain line of the backing fabric. Quilt with the lengthwise grain of the lining first, then quilt the crosswise or diagonal lines afterward. The quilt will remain square and much easier to control. This technique eliminates the drawing and stretching of

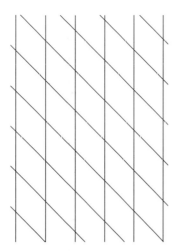

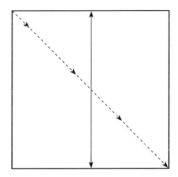

FIG. 11.15   Hanging diamond grid

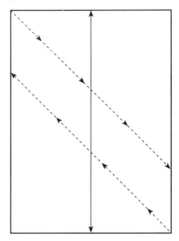

diagonal line will run from corner to corner (Figure 11.16). If the quilt is longer than it is wide, run two anchor lines diagonally, each one anchoring a different corner (Figure 11.17).

FIG. 11.17   Diagonal anchoring - rectangular quilt

FIG. 11.16   Diagonal anchoring - square quilt

the fabric between the stitching lines that occurs when working first with the bias, or stretchy crosswise grain.

Package the quilt for this example so that you can anchor the lengthwise center seam first. Next, anchor the diagonal direction so you will have anchor lines to cross as you quilt. If the quilt is square, this

Package the quilt so that you can quilt all lengthwise lines to the right of the center, top to bottom. Flip the quilt around, repackage, and quilt the seams from the right of the center, top to bottom. Now package the quilt diagonally, so that you are working from the center of the quilt out towards the corner. Flip the quilt around, and repackage so that you are repeating the process on the other half, working out to the corner. Throw these diagonal packages over your left shoulder to make them easier to work with.

Generally, this type of quilting extends into the border, so all that is left to do is trim, square and bind. It gets easier all the time!

Free-Motion Quilting Techniques

FREE-MOTION QUILTING WILL OPEN up a new world to you. I have no doubt that it will become your favorite method of machine quilting. It requires quite a bit of practice to master, but you will find the time well spent when you are able to reproduce beautiful quilting designs in minutes. What freedom you are allowed when the presser foot is removed! You can go forward, backward, side-to-side, in circles — anywhere you want to go — without ever turning the quilt. Specific techniques and detailed instructions are given for each method.

FREE-MOTION DESIGN QUILTING

Borders and plain blocks are a perfect place to show off fancy quilting (see Figure 12.1). Free-motion quilting gives the machine quilter the maneuverability needed to reproduce intricate designs used by hand quilters. Almost any hand quilting design can be done using free-motion methods. It gives you access to small designs, sharp curves and intricate patterns often very difficult to achieve by hand. After practicing and experimenting, you will also find yourself ditch quilting shorter lines with your darning foot.

FREE-MOTION EXERCISES — PLAIN FABRIC

After years of teaching machine quilting, I have found students have the most fun experimenting and playing with free-motion techniques. It is most helpful to have your sample practice blocks layered using 100% cotton batting because the layers stick together and eliminate the need for pinning. Your rhythm won't be broken by dodging pins or stopping to remove them.

Put the darning foot on your machine, and drop or cover your feed dogs, whichever your machine requires. Check your manual if you are unsure how to do this. Because the feed dogs are dropped, no stitch length adjustment is necessary. The stitch length is controlled by the speed in which you move the fabric under the foot, and the speed of the machine.

FIG. 12.1 Free-motion quilting

Get in the habit of always bringing the bobbin thread to the surface of the fabric before beginning to stitch (Figure 12.2). Review the starting process on page 70 if you need help. Be sure that both threads are under the darning foot, not coming up through the hole. Having both threads on top prevents them from jamming and snarling on the underside. Next, lower the needle into the hole where the bobbin thread is, and lower the presser bar (Figure 12.3).

Since no feeding is being done by the feed dogs, you will need to learn to move the fabric manually as you run the machine. This is where the concept "hand quilting with an electric needle" comes into play.

Your goal is to run the machine fairly fast. The faster you run the machine, the easier it is to develop accurate lines in your quilting. Practice on sample plain blocks. Find a comfortable speed and then keep it constant. Develop a rhythm with the

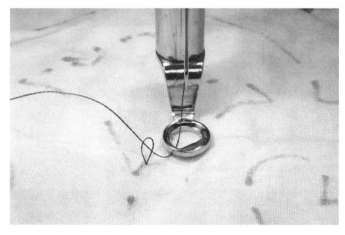

FIG. 12.2 Bring bobbin thread to top

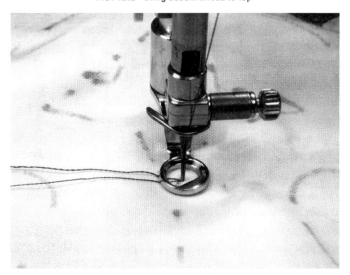

FIG. 12.3 Re-insert needle

motor speed of the machine. Do not gun the machine. Also do not go fast, then slow, then fast again. Erratic speed keeps your hands from developing a constant rhythm with the machine, and the quilting stitches will be ragged and uneven.

Start practicing by scribbling a design on a plain block. Pay attention to the speed of the machine, how your hands are moving the fabric under the needle, and the direction in which you need to move the fabric. Take a breath and relax! Think of it as drawing with the needle. You want a steady, flowing motion with the fabric with the machine running at a constant speed. If your machine has two motor speeds, try the slower one. This allows you to push the foot control all the way to the floor without going too fast and getting out of control.

Once you get a feel for the motion needed to move the fabric, start to move the fabric very slowly, side to side, and see what the stitch length looks like. Again, keep the machine at a constant speed. Begin to speed up the motion of your hands, but always keep the machine at the same speed. You should start to see the stitch length get longer and longer until eventually you are creating a basting stitch. Your sample should look similar to Figure 12.4 . This demonstrates how the stitch length is due totally to the motion of your hands, their consistency, and the speed of your machine. Refine the stitch length to the exact length you liked when using the walking foot. Eventually you will want all of your stitches to be the same length, regardless of the technique used.

FIG. 12.4 Stitch length variations

Here are some exercises to develop your skills. REMEMBER: Never turn the fabric, just glide it where you want it. Your hands need to be relaxed and your wrist kept up. Quilt with your fingertips, not your whole hand. This allows your fingers to gently walk the fabric where you want it. Use a gentle, sliding motion. If you ever played with a OUIJA® board, you know how to position your hands on the fabric. Too much pressure will cause the fabric to drag, making jerky, uneven movements. Try resting

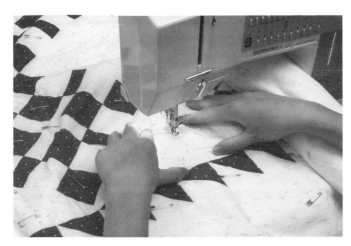

FIG. 12.5 Free-motion hand position

line. Do this by slowing the speed of the fabric, not the machine. You want to have ¼ inch of very tiny stitches at the beginning and end of every line as in ditch quilting. It may take practice to become accustomed to using different hand speeds while the machine is running at a constant speed. Repeat the lines below shown in Figure 12.8.

FIG. 12.8 Zigzag side to side

your forearms or elbows on the edge of the table. Then you can lean into the work, removing the tension from your shoulders and back. Again, a good chair is critical here. (See Figure 12.5).

When stitching forwards and backwards as seen in the illustration below, don't worry if the lines are not straight. For now, you are only concerned with the stitch length quality. Keep going up and down until you are able to keep the stitches fairly accurate (Figure 12.6).

Curves are next. Try drawing "e" and "l" shapes as though practicing penmanship. Keep practicing until the curves are smooth and free of points and ragged edges. Also try loops, circles and anything else you can think of (Figure 12.9).

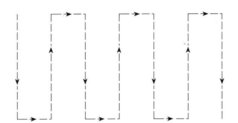

FIG. 12.6 Forward-backward exercises

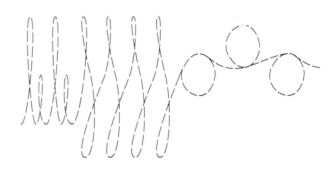

FIG. 12.9 Free-motion curves

Next, stitch side to side, left to right, back to the left, back to the right, etc. This will be foreign to you, as one generally does not sew sideways. Practice this until the stitches even out and become consistent (Figure 12.7).

Now you are ready to do zigzags. This time, lock off the stitches at the beginning and end of each

Continue by drawing stars, hearts, your name, pictures or anything else that comes to mind. Do not draw these images on the fabric; rather, visualize them and reproduce what you see in your head. The freedom you experience is like soaring! See Figures 12.10 and 12.11.

FIG. 12.7 Side to side exercises

FIG. 12.10 Free-motion images

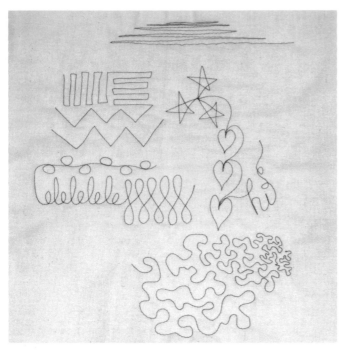

FIG. 12.11 Stitched sample

Once you feel you have control of the fabric and the stitch length, move on to a sample block. Draw a variety of continuous curve patterns on the block from the designs in the back of this book. Free drawing as above is fairly easy, but it becomes more difficult when you are contained to a given line. When practicing the techniques below, don't get too involved with the stitch length quality at first. It is very difficult to train yourself to stay on the line, let alone be able to keep the stitches accurate. This will all develop with time and practice. For now, concentrate on the lines and your eye placement.

Machine quilting lines takes a lot of concentration. While practicing, give yourself plenty of uninterrupted quiet time, and don't expect to quilt perfectly at first.

FREE-MOTION EXERCISES — DESIGNS

Trace a stencil or design onto the fabric exactly as it will be stitched. Start at the star on the pattern and work through the numbers in order. Finger trace the design several times until you become familiar with the "road" the needle will take.

Try this visualization exercise: Imagine yourself driving a car. You back out of the driveway, and as you start forward, you stare only at the hood ornament. If you do not look down the road, and you only stare at the hood ornament, where will you wind up? You have no control, and are flying blind. Now think of how you sew. If you only stare at the needle, not the line ahead of you, you have no idea of where the lines goes and what you need to do to get the line and the needle in the same place. You must know where you are going to get there successfully. After finger tracing the design, you know your "road." As you stitch, keep your eyes ahead of the needle, just as in driving, so that you know what to expect and can compensate for it. This will immediately improve your workmanship and control.

As you begin quilting, bring the bobbin thread up, hold onto both threads, and place the needle at the beginning of the line. Now, retrace the lines with your eyes so that you get used to the angle at which you are sitting and the light source. Lock off your stitching with very small stitches and cut the thread tails off. The secret to this is to not look at the needle or the hole inside the darning foot. Keep your eyes slightly ahead of the needle.

Remember your visualization experience. Quilt like you drive. Know where you are going before you get there. Your eyes will need to check on what you are doing, but only glance back and forth. Once you can do this, you will be able to stay on the line accurately and keep your stitches even. Practice and determination will enable you to do beautiful machine quilting in hours, instead of weeks or months. Practice, practice, practice.

If you are working with a design where you have to go from one area to another, do not cut the thread. Lock the threads, pull them across to the next area, lock them again at the beginning of the new line, and start stitching. After you finish with the design, clip all the extra threads.

TIP: If you find that you need to reposition your hands as you work through a design, stop with the needle in the down position. This will prevent the quilt from sliding and causing a loop of excess thread on the bottom of the quilt.

CONTINUOUS CURVE QUILTING

Continuous curve quilting is another form of free-motion quilting. I was introduced to this method several years ago by Barbara Johannah in her book,

FIG. 12.12 Continuous curve

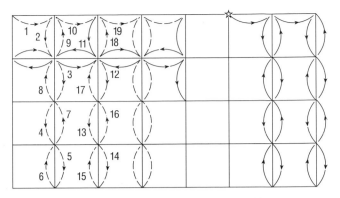

FIG. 12.13 Continuous curve system - grid

Continuous Curve Quilting. This method of quilting gives the look of hand outline quilting without the starting, stopping and turning of the quilt under the needle to achieve traditional straight lines (Figure 12.12). Gentle arcs replace all of the straight lines and corners. The arcs go from corner to corner, with the deepest point ¼ inch in from the seam at the center point of the line.

I took Barbara's idea one step further by using the darning foot. This eliminates the need for the turning that is necessary when working with a walking or regular foot. The darning foot allows you to go sideways, forward, and backward without turning and rotating. It also speeds up the process and allows all pieces in the block to be quilted.

CONTINUOUS CURVE EXERCISES

Plan your block strategy on graph paper. Start in an outside corner, trace through the block, and attempt to follow every side of every piece without stopping. Use gentle arcs from corner to corner. Other designs require you to start in the center of the block or along the side. See examples in Figures 12.13 and 12.14.

If you follow the arrows in Figure 12.13 you can see how the line snakes from side to side to accommodate each side of each piece, instead of using short, jerky scalloped lines on the same side of each

block. This procedure allows a fluid motion with your hands as you weave the line from side to side. Figure 12.14 starts inside the block and works out in a rotating manner.

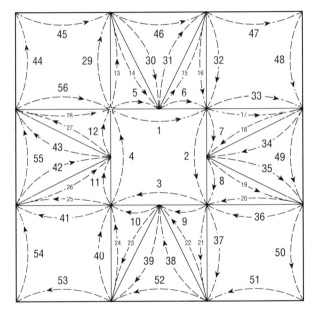

FIG. 12.14 Continuous curve system - star

In Figure 12.15 a long border of triangles is quilted by continually stitching only two sides of each triangle, then stitching back in a scallop motion to finish all of the third sides.

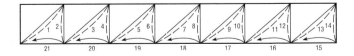

FIG. 12.15 Continuous curve system - triangle border

When you get comfortable with the feel of free-motion quilting, you will be able to "eyeball" the curves and just sew without marking. Until then, you may need to make a set of templates for these curves, and mark the lines on the quilt top to use as a guide. At the very least, mark a dot at the center point where the line goes into a piece the deepest.

To make the templates, draw a square, triangle or whatever shape you are working with onto a piece of graph paper the finished size of the piece. Using a french curve or a flexi-curve, connect two corners to make the arc. Be sure that the deepest part of the arc is in the center of the line and no more than ¼ inch deep. Make a complete set of templates for all the different sizes in the patchwork pieces. Use plastic to make a permanent set (Figures 12.16 and 12.17).

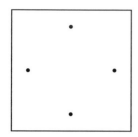

FIG. 12.16　¼ inch guide dots at center points

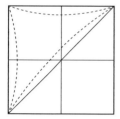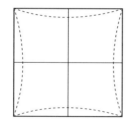

FIG. 12.17　Continuous curve templates

ECHO QUILTING

Echo quilting is the repeating of a shape or design as you move out from it, eventually distorting the lines somewhat (Figure 12.18). Similar to the ripples created by dropping a pebble into a pool of water, the lines distort a little more as they go away from the design. Use this technique for appliqué designs, as well as silk-screened and stenciled fabrics, because it sets off the design well.

ECHO QUILTING EXERCISES

Echo quilting can also be done by free-motion quilting with a darning foot. When first experimenting, you may want to lightly draw the quilting lines onto the fabric to get the feel of the design and to mark guidelines. After awhile, you will find that doing it

FIG. 12.18　Echo quilting

free-form under the needle is fun because you can see the interesting shapes develop as you stitch.

To begin, bury some tiny straight stitches in the ditch of your design or appliqué. The first quilting is done in the ditch around all edges of the design. Keep your eye on the needle. You do not want this stitching to show at all so the design will rise above the surface and have more puff.

The next line starts the echo process. Use the edge of your darning foot to measure the distance from the edge of the appliqué. This will make the line about ¼ inch outside the edge of the design. Work clockwise around the design, repeating every detail of the appliqué edge. As you come back to the beginning stitching, lock off the stitches again. Now move the foot out so that its edge is against the line you just completed. This will measure the next ¼ inch line out, and will expand the design. Continue this process until you are to the edge of the block. Eventually you will reach the outer edges and run off the fabric. Continue stitching into the corners until the entire block is "echoed." When you get to the outer seam, you can move to the next position by stitching in the ditch of the seam instead of locking off the thread. The seams become "highways" that allow you to get from one place to another without breaking the thread.

Printed panels, border prints, stenciled designs, and large prints can easily be quilted using this technique. The quilting can be as general as outlining the larger designs or as intricate as outlining every detail. Panel prints are ideal for practicing.

STIPPLE QUILTING

Stippling is a form of echo quilting. Originally it was done very close. Like even echo stitching, it fills in an entire area and creates a heavily quilted texture. Stippling is most often seen on antique counterpanes, but seldom on modern quilts because of the great amount of time needed to accomplish the process by hand.

Machine stippling, also known as meandering, is commonly used for background fill work. The stitching looks random at first glance, but when examined closely, you see that the lines never touch each other, nor do they cross or look scribbled (Figure 12.20). They are very controlled, curly lines that systematically fill in both large and small areas with an abundance of texture. Stipple quilting can be very tiny or very large and open. Stipple techniques on the machine should not resemble echo quilting, but should appear totally random and free.

Machine stippling is an excellent way to develop the skills of free-motion quilting, but it requires a lot of practice. Remember to look ahead and visualize what you are trying to draw. You may need to sit

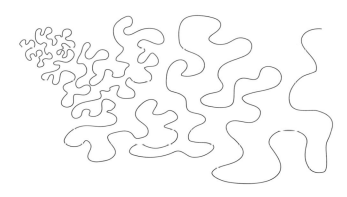

FIG. 12.20 Stipple quilting

with a piece of paper and doodle for a while to get the feel of the motion. Figure 12.20 shows a line drawing of stippling in various sizes.

When working a background with stippling, try not to get cornered. Plan the work so that it is very random and goes into every area continuously. Use the corners and points of the design to get in and out of the area.

Next I will give you guidelines for quilting larger quilts using free-motion techniques.

FREE-MOTION QUILTING EXERCISES

Double Irish Chain

Many quilts do not need ditch quilting. Straight lines may appear too harsh and stiff for the quilt's overall appearance. Ditch quilting might break into a secondary design developed by the patchwork, causing confusion when viewing the finished quilt.

FIG. 12.19 Stipple quilting

FIG. 12.21 Double Irish Chain

The Double Irish Chain baby quilt on page 83 is an example of such a quilt top.

Ditch quilting between the blocks of this quilt would create a straight-line depression in what seems to be a diagonally appearing quilt. Long, straight diagonal lines through the double chain squares would appear too rigid and stiff. Therefore, ditch quilting is not appropriate for this top.

The design for this quilting pattern can be done totally with the darning foot in very little time. There is no need to use the anchoring system. Because the darning foot does not use the feed dogs, there is no pushing and pulling on the fabric from a feeding system. Use the same order for the quilting progress, but eliminate the first two steps for the anchoring lines.

Quilt this quilt block-by-block, row-by-row. Each block is completed as you go down the row. The 5-patch pieced block, block "A", is quilted with a zig-zag pattern in a side-to-side movement. Either draw these lines onto the fabric, or eyeball them as you go. See Figure 12.22.

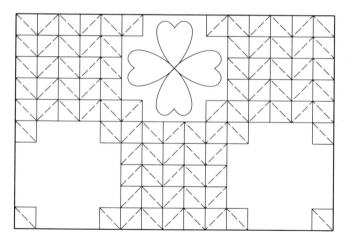

FIG. 12.22 Quilting illustration

Package the quilt so that the center row of blocks is exposed. Start with the first block in the row, the first row of the block. Position the needle into the fabric at the top left corner of the first square. Stitch toward the bottom right corner of that square, then continue up to the right top corner of the next square, the bottom right corner of the next, etc. (Figure 12.23).

Once that row is completed, lock off the stitches and pull the thread down to the next row. The needle will be placed in the first block on the right side

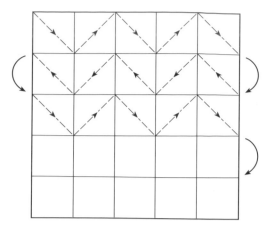

FIG. 12.23 Quilting system for 'A' block

of the second row. Do not cut the threads until you have locked off the stitches again. Lock off and start stitching to the left. With the needle in the lower right corner, stitch to the upper left corner of that square, down to the lower left corner of the next square, etc. Continue this process until all five rows are completed. NOTE: The corner squares of the "B" block will be combined with the "A" block when they align in the same rows.

Pull the thread into the center area of the connector "B" block, and quilt the design motif you have selected. Continue with the next "A" block. Once this row of blocks is completed, repackage the quilt for the next row of blocks to the right. Repeat the above process. When all rows to the right are finished, flip the quilt around so that the unquilted side is to your right. Repackage and repeat the process with this side. Quilt the borders last, then square and bind. You'll be amazed how fast you get the quilting finished when you use the darning foot.

Nine-Patch and Hourglass

The Nine-Patch and Hourglass quilt presents a real challenge to machine quilting. Although there are a lot of straight lines, the use of a walking foot is not practical. Again, consider how many times you would need to start and stop or slightly turn the quilt. That makes the quilting difficult and time-consuming, and encourages distortion and puckering.

Each block is quilted separately as shown in Figures 12.24 and 12.25. Package the quilt to expose the center row of blocks. Quilt the four inner squares of the 9-patch block in a spiraling motion. Work from the outside edge in to the center of the square. Do not quilt the diagonal lines yet. Next,

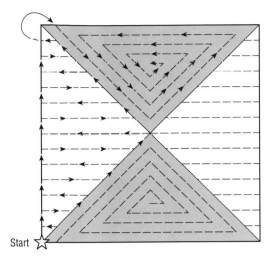

FIG. 12.24 Quilting lines for connecting block

FIG. 12.25 Quilting lines for nine-patch

move on to the connector block. Half of the block can be done at a time without breaking the thread. Begin in one corner of the triangle with straight lines. Work up and down the lines, using the ditches as highways, until you are at the opposite corner and all straight lines are finished (see Figure 12.25). Slip into the ditch and move into the dark triangle. Begin the inward spiral, locking off when you get to the innermost region. Pull the thread to the next light triangle and stitch with straight lines. Repeat the above process. This will allow you to quilt the entire connector block with only one thread break. Repeat for the four inner square spirals on the next block in the row, etc.

Once this process has been completed for the entire quilt, you are ready to quilt the parallel diagonal lines through the 9-patches. Use the darning foot to eliminate turning the quilt to accommodate the corners of the adjoining blocks. The ditches become "highways" again, to get from one square to the

next, without stitching on top of the corner (see Figure 12.26).

Package the quilt for the diagonal lines (refer to page 68 for this information.) Using the darning foot, quilt to the end of the line of the first square, glide into the ditch, and stitch in the ditch first one direction, then the other, then out again onto the diagonal line of the next square. Continue in this manner the distance of the total line, border to border. You can either quilt the parallel line next to the one just quilted backwards with the darning foot, or you can lock off the stitches and re-position the quilt to go forwards down the line.

The traditional fan pattern in the border is also simple to quilt with the darning foot. Each fan is done as a unit, following the line of the next to get from one row to another (see Figure 12.27).

This quilt can be quilted in approximately 14 hours using the darning foot. If you use a walking foot, you easily double the time investment and the stress level!

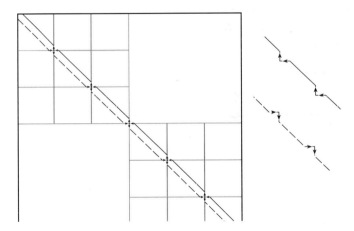

FIG. 12.26 Continuous lines through nine-patch

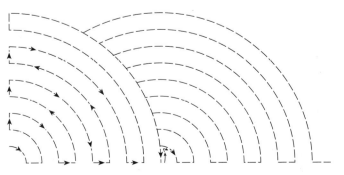

FIG. 12.27 Continuous stitching fans

MEDALLION QUILTS

Lone Star

The Lone Star quilt pictured in the color section on page 46 is one of my favorites. Most quilters make a Lone Star at one time or another and it is usually ditch quilted. Ditch quilting is boring to do and boring to look at. I chose Barbara Johannah's continuous curve methods to quilt this quilt, and found it to be a delightful experience.

Medallions are more difficult to handle than straight and diagonal set quilts, and the system you have used up to now does not apply. Medallion quilts need to be quilted from the center out following the general dispersion of the pattern. Therefore, instead of a neat, tidy package, the quilt is opened up and free, making it easier to rotate the quilt to follow the circular pattern.

The Lone Star is made up of eight points. Each point shares a common pivot point, the center, where all eight points meet. Each point is made up of 4 to 6 rows, 4 to 6 diamonds to a row. You have two options for containing as much bulk as possible. You can quilt each ring created by the points in a circular motion. But as you get out further into the star, you are moving a lot of fabric to follow the pattern.

The other method, which I prefer, breaks the star down into points, and you work one point at a time.

FIG. 12.28 Lone Star continuous curve

Package the quilt as neatly as possible. You will find that it needs to be opened up quite a bit to accommodate the size of the star point. The package will be messy and more awkward than with previous quilts. Start with the center pivot point. Move to the right, into the first row of the first point. Stitch a continuous curve line from the pivot point to the top right corner, stitch down the right side of the first diamond, back up the first side of the second diamond, across the top of the second, down the right side, up the left side of the third diamond, across the top and down the right side, etc. (Figure 12.29).

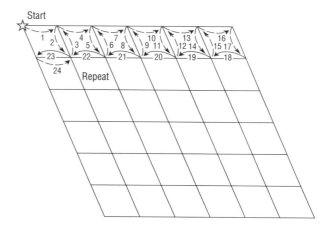

FIG. 12.29 Continuous curve system

Once you are at the end of row one, come back toward the center pivot point, stitching the curved line along the bottom side of each diamond on the first row. Do not go back up to the pivot point; instead, repeat this process for the second row of diamonds.

Continue this process until all rows of the first point are finished. Come back to the pivot point by stitching the curved lines up the side of the point, into the pivot point (Figure 12.30). Now you are ready to rotate the entire quilt until the first row of the second point is lined up to your right. Repeat as you did for point one.

This process eliminates the need to constantly lock off and cut threads. The only time this is necessary is when you run out of bobbin thread.

Ohio Rose

The Ohio Rose quilt pictured on page 44 is a good example of echo quilting. To begin, package the quilt so that the center row of appliqué blocks is exposed. Start quilting in the ditch around the

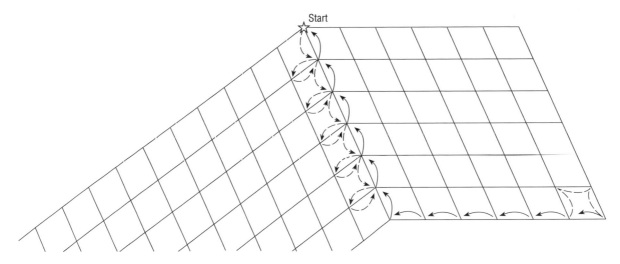

FIG. 12.30 Starting second point

appliqué, free-motion with a darning foot. You will need to guide the block so that the needle runs along the edge of each appliqué piece. This is also a good time to do the inside surface quilting of each petal and leaf. With a small amount of double-stitching in certain ditches, this can all be done in one continuous motion.

FIG. 12.31 Ditch and outline quilting

Proceed to the echo quilting. Let the edge of the darning foot ride along the ridge of the appliqué pieces. This will measure the distance consistently around the entire appliqué. Continue around the appliqué until you meet the point where you started. This should give you a quilting line approximately ¼ inch from the edge of the appliqué around the block. Repeat this procedure allowing the edge of the darning foot to follow the quilting line that you just finished. Continue doing this until the echo lines reach the seamline of the block (Figure 12.32). Go to the next block and repeat. Repeat the process until all appliqué blocks are quilted to their seamlines.

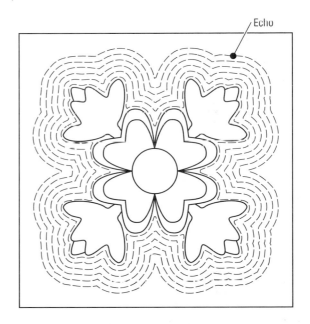

FIG. 12.32 Echo quilting

Once each block is echoed to the seam line, you will see that there are "puddles" left between each block (Figure 12.33). Quilt these areas by working from the previously quilted lines, working in to the center of each puddle. Each round of quilting will be separate, not continuous. Remember to lock the stitches well at the beginning and end of every line.

Once all the blocks are quilted, you are ready to move into the border. Crosshatch quilting is very effective on this quilt, as shown in the picture on page 44. The border layers may shift or become distorted if great care is not taken. Approach the border from the centers out. Start at the border seamline and stitch out toward the raw edge. Stitch all lines of the same direction first, starting in the center of the border and progressing to the corner. Repeat this for

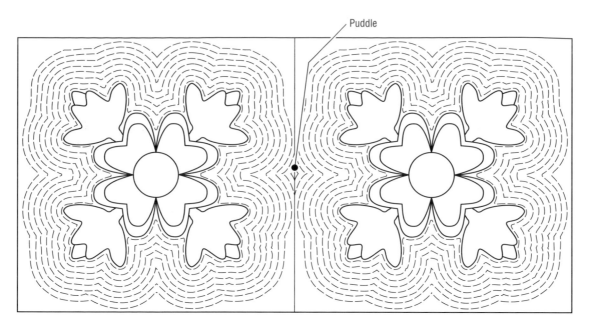

Puddle

FIG. 12.33 Echo quilting puddle

the other half of the border. Once the entire border is quilted once, repeat the process and do the crossing lines. Use your hands, and be careful that the fabric does not "draw" between the quilting lines; it should lie flat and smooth.

The quilts shown here exemplify the various approaches to machine quilting. Every quilt will be slightly different, but general rules seem to always apply to help you create a beautiful quilt by machine.

Combining Ditch and Free-Motion Quilting

THE AMISH SHADOWS QUILT below in (Figures 13.1 and 13.2) is a perfect example of combining techniques. The quilt is sewn together with straight set blocks, but each block has a diagonal seam. Within one half of each block are four shorter seams. The opposite side is blank, leaving space for a fancy design.

Start by quilting in the two anchor lines, one lengthwise and one crosswise. Continue with the system, until all straight lines are quilted. Now repackage so that you can quilt the long, continuous diagonal lines that run through the center of each block. Work from the center to the right corner of each side (see Figures 13.3 and 13.4).

Move on to the short, inner seams of each block. Use the darning foot and free-motion ditch quilt

FIG. 13.2 Block closeup

FIG. 13.1 Amish Shadows

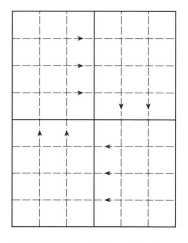

FIG. 13.3 Ditch quilting straight lines

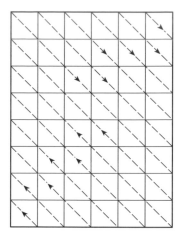

FIG. 13.4 Ditch quilting diagonal lines

these lines. This eliminates the need to constantly move from one block to the next and lock and cut all the threads (Figure 13.5).

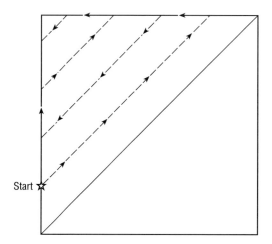

FIG. 13.5 Free-motion ditch quilting

With the darning foot, you can sew forwards, backwards, sideways, at angles, and in any direction you need to go, without turning the quilt or starting and stopping. The side ditches have already been quilted in the first process, but no harm is done by quilting them again. I use these ditches as highways to get from one place to another without breaking the thread.

It will take some practice to be able to put the needle where you want it all the time (on the low side), but perseverance will pay big dividends in speed and quality.

Star Chain, pictured on page 44, is another quilt that is a combination of ditch and free-motion quilt-

ing. Anytime a quilt can be ditch quilted without the stitching lines detracting from the desired surface texture, do it. This type of anchoring makes it easier to work with the larger areas in free-motion quilting. The layers are less likely to move and become distorted once they are stitched between the blocks.

On Star Chain, begin by anchoring the diagonal center seams. (Refer to page 68 for information on handling a diagonal set.) Stitch the first center diagonal seamline, repackage, and repeat for the opposite diagonal line. This will create an "X" through the center of the quilt. After anchoring, continue stitching each side from each anchor line, center to the right toward each corner. Repackage for each line.

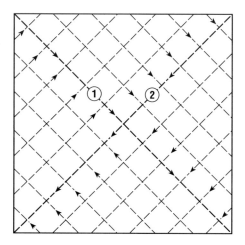

FIG. 13.6 Anchoring and ditch quilting

Once ditch stitched, repackage so that a "row" of blocks is exposed, and begin quilting down the row, one at a time, top to bottom. Complete all stitching that needs to be done within each block as you go. Once that row is completed, unroll the right side to expose the next row of blocks, fold up the left side, and repeat the process. Continue until all of the rows to the right are completed. Turn the quilt around, repackage, and repeat the process for the other side of the quilt. Quilt the borders and you are finished.

By now, all this information should affect your way of thinking. Look at your collection of quilts and quilt tops, and imagine how you might machine quilt each project.

Finishing Up

Binding

ONCE THE QUILT IS COMPLETELY QUILTED, you are ready to trim the edges, square the corners, and apply the binding. Binding causes most quilters to groan, but once you know the tricks that make it easy, it no longer seems such a dreadful task.

After you complete the quilting, clip all stray threads and check for any missed quilting lines or loose stitches. Trim the edges and square the corners into perfect 90° angles.

HALF-INCH BINDING

If you want to finish your quilt with a traditional ½-inch binding, trim the quilt so that you have a little less than ¼-inch batting and lining beyond the edge of the top. This fills the width of the binding which extends beyond the seam allowance. When wrapping the binding around the edge, be sure the binding is filled to the edge with the quilt to prevent excess wear on the folded edge.

Straight-grain binding is preferred over bias binding when binding a straight-edge quilt; it keeps the quilt edge straight with no ripples. A bias binding is "stretchy" and may give the quilt a stretched appearance along the edge. The quilt appears to ripple when hung or placed on a bed. Use bias binding only when a quilt has rounded corners or scallops.

NOTE: The argument for bias is that the edge does not wear as badly because there is not a single thread in the weave that runs along the edge as in straight-grain binding. My argument here is that when I cut my crosswise strips to make the binding, I fold the selvages to the folded edge, and 99% of the time, the grain is off on the bolt. Therefore, the strips are not perfectly on grain, yet they are not true bias. This gives me the best of both methods, since the grain is slightly off, allowing more threads to take the wear, but it is not nearly as stretchy as bias.

Cut the binding strips 2½ inches wide. You can use lengthwise or crosswise grain. Crosswise grain has a slight amount of stretch, so be careful not to stretch it when applying it to the edge of the quilt. Do not mix strips cut from both grains. The color will appear to be different, and the fabric will behave differently.

Measure the outer edge of the quilt to find the total length of binding required. Add 12 inches to this measurement. You will need about ⅔ yard of fabric to produce the 30 feet of binding needed to go around a quilt 80 inches by 90 inches. Cut 9 strips of fabric, each measuring 2½ inches wide by 45 inches long (if using the crosswise width). Cut each end of the strip at a 45° angle (bias) (Figure 14.1). Join these strips using a bias seam (Figure 14.2).

Keep joining the strips with the right sides together until you have a continuous piece of binding (Figure 14.3). Strips are joined together this way so that when they are applied to the quilt, the layers from the seams won't stack up and leave a lump. Instead, the seams spiral to distribute the bulk evenly.

FIG. 14.1   Binding

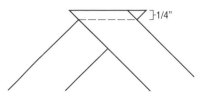

FIG. 14.2   Binding

Press the seams open. Fold the 2½-inch strip in half, lengthwise, making a strip 1¼ inches wide. Starting in the center of one side of the quilt, lay the raw edges of the binding on the raw edge of the quilt top. Begin sewing, leaving about 8 inches of the strip free behind the foot for joining later. Stitch ¼ inch from the raw edge down the length of the quilt.

When approaching a corner, stop stitching ¼ inch from the edge. (Figure 14.4).

TIP: Check to see if the bar in front of your needle on the presser foot measures ¼ inch. Many do, and this is an excellent way to know when to stop.

Leaving the needle in the fabric, turn the quilt 90° so that you are ready to stitch down the next edge. Instead of sewing forward, backstitch off the edge (Figures 14.4 and 14.5).

Fold the binding straight up, away from the corner, to form a 45° angle fold (Figure 14.6). Bring the binding straight down in line with the next side to be sewn (Figure 14.7). The fold must rest along the top edge of the quilt, and the two folded edges on the left should be exactly aligned. Do not skimp on this fold or the miter will not be accurate. Begin stitching the next side at the top of the fold, stitching through all thicknesses. Miter each corner in this manner.

As you approach the starting point, stop about 16 inches from the beginning stitches. This allows plenty of room to join the ends on the bias. Overlap the loose ends of binding where they meet. Lay the ends of the side 2 binding strip flat, and lay the beginning end of side 1 on top of side 2, keeping both binding strips folded. Label the long point of side 1

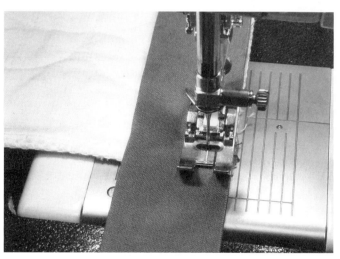

FIG. 14.4   Stop ¼ inch from ends

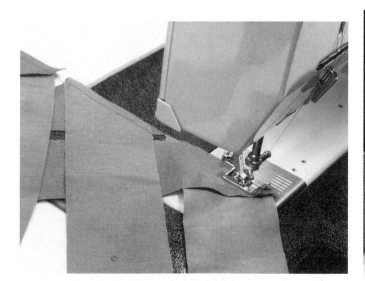

FIG. 14.3   Joining strip ends

FIG. 14.5   Backstitch off edge

"A". Label the short point of side 1 "B" (Figures 14.8 and 14.9).

Mark dot A onto the top layer of side 2. Mark dot B onto the bottom layer of side 2 (Figure 14.10).

Open side 2 and measure ½ inch to the left of these dots. This provides seam allowances. Cut on this line (Figure 14.11).

Open side 1. With right sides together, stitch side 1 to side 2 using a ¼-inch seam allowances (Figure 14.12).

Press the seam open. Fold the joined strip in half and press. The binding should be a perfect fit. Finish stitching binding to the edge of the quilt.

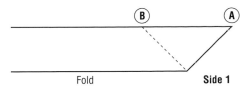

FIG. 14.8 Labeling side one

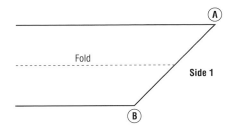

FIG. 14.9 Labeling side one

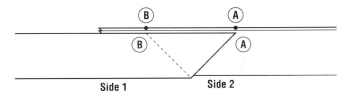

FIG. 14.10 Marking side two

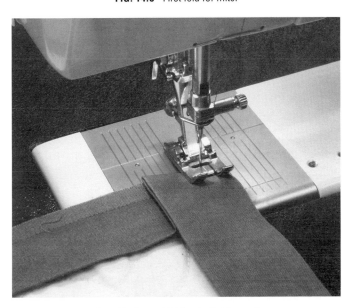

FIG. 14.6 First fold for miter

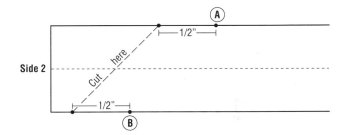

FIG. 14.11 Cutting end of side two

FIG. 14.12 Stitching ends together

FIG. 14.7 Second fold and stitching on top

Wrap the binding over the raw edge to the back of the quilt. Fold under, and place the folded edge of the binding on top of the stitching line. Sew a very tiny blindstitch to secure the binding. A blindstitch should be no longer than ¼ inch and should not show on the front or back. If properly stitched, the blindstitch gives an almost invisible finish. Slide the needle through the folded edge and at the same point, pick up one or two threads of the lining fabric. Continue doing this, taking stitches ⅛ to ¼ inch apart. Space the stitches evenly (Figure 14.13).

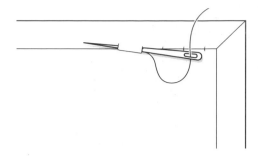

FIG. 14.13 Finishing the edge

A perfect miter at the corner is already formed on the top of the quilt. On the back, form a miter and continue to secure with blindstitching. The fold of this miter should be the opposite direction from the one on the right side, so the bulk of the miter will be evenly distributed (Figure 14.14 and 14.15).

FIG. 14.14 Finished corner – front side

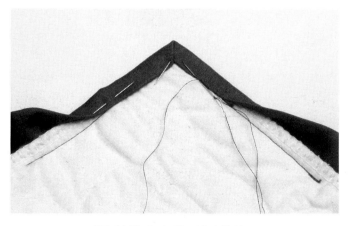

FIG. 14.15 Back side – blindstitching

1-INCH BORDER BINDING

The 1-inch border binding is fun and fast. The wide finished binding also serves as a small border or frame for the quilt.

Cut strips 5½ inches wide. If you need additional length to make the border for one side of the quilt, join strips on the bias as described under ½-inch binding (Figures 14.1 and 14.2). Do not join all the strips together this time as you did for ½-inch binding. The strips should be 5 to 6 inches longer than each side of the quilt. Fold the strips in half lengthwise, making them 2¾ inches wide, and press.

To prepare the quilt top, trim the backing and batting to ¾ inch beyond the edge of the quilt top. This will be enclosed within the binding. Sew the binding onto one side of the quilt top, starting and stopping ¼ inch from the raw edge (the seam line) that is perpendicular to the edge you are sewing (Figure 14.16).

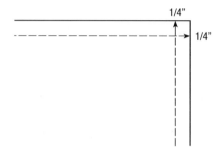

FIG. 14.16 Sew ¼ inch from raw edges

A 2½- to 3-inch tail of binding has been left at each end of each border strip. Now join these tails at the corners to make perfect miters by folding one edge's tail back so that it lies perfectly on the binding (see arrow in Figure 14.17). Lay the other side over it. Draw a line on the top piece that extends the seam line of the binding piece that is on the bottom. This line is AB (Figure 14.17).

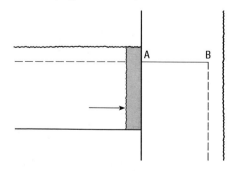

FIG. 14.17 Preparing corner

Find the measurement that is halfway between the folded edge and the seam line of AB. C is the midpoint of line AB. Draw a line from C that is at a right angle to AB (perpendicular). On this line, measure up from C the same distance as AC or CB. This point is D. Example: If AC = 1¼ inches, CB should = 1¼ inches and CD should = 1¼ inches.

Draw in a sewing line that goes from A to D and D to B (Figure 14.18).

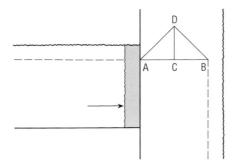

FIG. 14.18 Developing sewing line

Open both sides of the binding and fold the quilt diagonally from the corner. Align both binding strips so that their edges are exactly even and their corners match. Pin in place and sew line ADB. Backstitch at the beginning and end. At the point, you might need to take a stitch across the point to keep it perfect. Stop stitching one stitch from the point, take one stitch across to the other side, and continue down line DB (see Figures 14.19, 14.20, and 14.21).

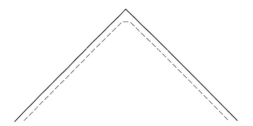

FIG. 14.19 One stitch across triangle tip

FIG. 14.20 Marking triangle

FIG. 14.21 Stitched and trimmed

Use a point turner to straighten the point and roll the binding to the back. The folded edge should align with the seam line on the back, making a perfect mitered corner on the front and back. Stitch in place by hand or machine (Figure 14.22).

FIG. 14.22 Finished corner

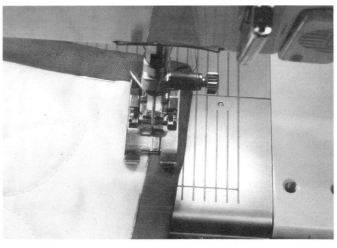

FIG. 14.23 Finishing by ditch stitching

Binding can be finished from the top with the machine by ditch stitching with matching or nylon thread. Roll the binding to the back, with the fold just slightly beyond the stitching line. With pin heads toward you, pin the binding in the ditch on the top side of the quilt. To stitch in place, guide the machine needle exactly in the ditch, removing the pins as you come to them. No stitching should show on the top, and the binding edge should just be caught by the stitches on the back (Figure 14.23). If finishing by hand, use a blindstitch.

Care and Keeping

NOW THAT YOUR WORK IS FINISHED, proper care and storage of your quilt will ensure years of joy, beauty and pride. A machine pieced and quilted quilt is not as fragile as one pieced and quilted by hand. It will probably be used more, but we make quilts to use, enjoy, and share.

LAUNDERING YOUR NEW QUILTS

There seems to be a lot of anxiety about caring for quilts whether they are new or antique! Quilters overlook the fact that the soil trapped in the fibers can often cause more damage than the actual laundering process. Textiles are more sensitive to light, airborne dust, pollution and stains than most other art objects. Consider what the fabric has been exposed to during construction: body oil from your hands, lint from being handled, soil from being on the floor a few times. No wonder the quilt is usually quite soiled upon finishing.

Start the cleaning process by vacuuming. This will remove dust particles whose sharp edges start to eat away at the fibers. Buy a two-foot-square piece of fiberglass screening and bind the edges with twill tape. Place the screen on the quilt. Using the corner attachment of the vacuum, gently vacuum over the screen, cleaning the front and the back of the quilt.

A bath is needed to remove dirt and stains, but washing can permanently damage the quilt if care is not taken. Test for colorfastness in today's cottons whether you prewash your new fabrics or not. Many quilts have bled when they were washed the first time even though the fabrics were prewashed. This is often irreversible. With care, the fabrics used in the quilt can look as fresh and new after the first laundering as they did before.

Choose a safe washing agent for cleaning your quilts. A general rule of thumb that I use is that the product needs to be something I would be willing to take a bath in. This automatically eliminates general laundry detergents which can cause bleeding, fading, and rapid aging of cotton fabrics. Highly recommended products are Orvus Paste, Easy Wash® and Mountain Mist Ensure®. Orvus Paste is recommended overall because it is a neutral product that rinses out of the quilt thoroughly.

Color testing should be done for every fabric in the quilt, not just the ones you might think could bleed. (Remember, if the quilt bleeds in washing, it

FIG. 15.1 Care products

could be irreversible, and prewashing should not be relied on solely for colorfastness.) If you have seven different blues in the quilt, test all seven. Start by rubbing a dry, white cloth gently over each fabric to see if any color rubs off. If not, dampen the cloth with cool tap water and rub it over the fabric. If no color appears, the next step is to use warm water, and if that is safe, use warm water with the diluted washing agent you have chosen. I generally mix 1 teaspoon Orvus to 1 quart of warm water.

If any of the fabrics bleed, do not wash the quilt. I have had experiences where the detergent was not safe, and bleeding occurred. This needs to be treated immediately because the bleeding can be permanent if the quilt is allowed to dry. I have had excellent results with Easy Wash, a soil and stain remover for natural fibers. Fill the washer with cold water and add ¾ to 1 cup of Easy Wash concentrate. Soak the quilt in this solution for 15 minutes. (Easy Wash can be applied directly to stained areas as well.) Rinse and check for fading. If the color is gone, proceed to drying. If the color is still apparent, repeat the process. Snowy Bleach® is another product that removes excess color when bleeding has occurred. These products are by no means guaranteed to solve the problem, but they do have a good track record.

If the color tests show that the fabrics do not bleed, you can proceed with the washing. (We are discussing the care of new quilts here, not antiques. Consult a textile conservator concerning the care of antique quilts of value.) I launder my quilts in the washing machine.

Fill the washer to its largest capacity with warm water. A rule of thumb is to use the temperature you bathe a baby in. Add the Orvus or your chosen washing agent and agitate to dissolve. Turn the washer off and gently add the quilt. Completely immerse the quilt and let it soak for ten minutes. Then using your hands, gently move the quilt in the water to release the soil from the fabric. Do this for about five minutes. Detergent has the ability to clean for only 12 to 15 minutes. If the water is very soiled, you will need to repeat this process until the quilt appears clean. (Soaking in the same water for a long period of time will not get the quilt clean.)

Spin the water out of the quilt on the gentle spin cycle. Spinning will not harm the quilt, and is much easier on the fibers than handling a heavy, dripping wet quilt. NOTE: This method is not recommended for king-size quilts. Extra large front-loading washers are recommended for laundering any large spread or quilt.

To rinse, carefully remove the quilt from the washer and fill the tub with warm water. Keep the water temperature for washing and rinsing the same. Place the quilt in the water and gently move it around to remove the washing agent from the fibers. Drain the water and spin. If possible, watch as the water drains from the tube. If soapy residue continues to come from the water, rinse again. The water should run completely clear at the end of the cycle to indicate that the quilt is thoroughly rinsed. This may take as many as five rinsings, depending on the washing agent and amount of detergent used.

There are differing opinions on how to dry a quilt, but do not put a wet quilt in the clothes dryer! The tumbling action is hard on the quilt. It can also cause crocking — the surface loss of color by friction — and streaking of the fabric colors. I think the best way to dry a quilt is to lay it flat. I prefer to dry quilts outdoors on a dry, breezy, sunny day. I use sheets — one on the ground and one on top of the quilt — to protect it from insects and sun. Grommets can be put in the corners of the sheets so they can be staked down to prevent blowing in the breeze. When the quilt is dry to the touch, turn it over to dry the other side. I have also had success drying quilts over large bushes. Cover the bush with a sheet, lay the quilt over the bush, and cover with another sheet. The bush allows the quilt to be off the ground, yet provides total support and air circulation.

If you need to dry indoors, lay the quilt on the floor, using sheeting or plastic to protect the floor. Oscillating fans will speed the drying process considerably. Creating a large drying screen from a piece of mosquito netting, fiberglass screen, etc., can also be helpful in getting the quilt off the floor and aiding air circulation. Never hang a wet quilt as the pressure of hanging can weaken the fabrics and tear the stitches. If you want to fluff the quilt a bit when it is barely damp dry, place it in the dryer on air or fluff — no heat.

Remember to use the most natural ways to wash and store your treasured quilts. Go back and think about the old ways of doing things. Our grandmothers had more common sense than we seem to have. Our harsh chemicals and push-button machines have caused many things to be ruined.

STORING QUILTS IN THE HOME

When not in use, quilts should be carefully stored. We tend to think that only old or antique quilts need special care and consideration. However, if new quilts are to remain beautiful and damage-free in the years to come, you need to consider how they are cared for today. The most ideal way to store quilts is unfolded, flat, and unstacked. However, few of us have the luxury of this kind of space.

Avoid storing quilts, or any textiles for that matter, in attics or basements. Attics are too hot and basements are too damp. Ideal temperatures are between 60° and 70°F. Humidity levels need to be between 45% and 60%. Humidity is the real killer for quilts, causing mold and mildew problems. Quilts should be stored within the living area of your home, preferably away from outside walls, and in an area that is dark most of the time, but that provides some air circulation. A good guideline is that if the temperature and humidity level are comfortable to you, it will also be good for your quilts.

Avoid using plastic bags. Plastic cuts off air circulation and emits harmful by-products as it ages. The static electricity generated by plastics attracts dust, which is also undesirable. Finally, mold and mildew result from moisture trapped inside plastic bags. If you see little black spots on a quilt, which indicate mildew, very little can be done. (Mildew can also be detected by the odor.) Prevent mildew with good air circulation.

Use well-washed cotton muslin sheeting or acid-free tissue paper to protect quilts from wood surfaces, dust, light and abrasion. Fabric wrappings can be washed once a year; tissue paper needs to be changed at least that often.

FOLDED STORAGE

Storing a folded quilt presents a major problem. Fold lines create stress on the quilted fabric, stitches and batting. You can reduce this stress by padding the folded areas with tissue paper or cotton

sheeting. Lay the quilt out on a clean, flat surface. Place a sheet of acid-free tissue paper on the center of the quilt. Make a crumpled roll and place it across the quilt so that the top ⅓ of the quilt can be folded over the roll. Place another roll of paper across the lower ⅓ of the quilt, and fold the lower third over the roll. Now the quilt is folded in thirds. Place a shorter roll of paper across the folded quilt ⅓ of the way in. Fold the left side towards the center. Repeat with the right side. Avoid stacking quilts if possible, as this counteracts the tissue paper padding (see Figures 15.2 through 15.10).

Once the quilt has been folded, it is ready for storage. Acid-free boxes are a good choice if your space is limited and you need to stack the quilts. A box keeps stress off the quilt directly, but it does reduce air circulation.

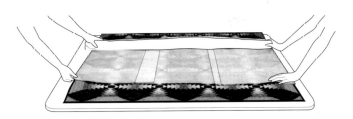

FIG. 15.2 Tissue roll for top third of quilt

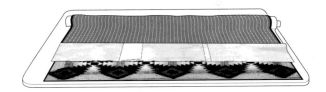

FIG. 15.3 Top third folded over roll

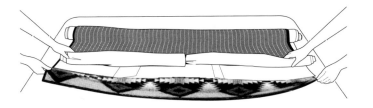

FIG. 15.4 Tissue roll for bottom third

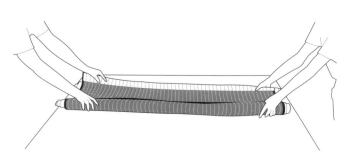

FIG. 15.5   Bottom third folded over roll

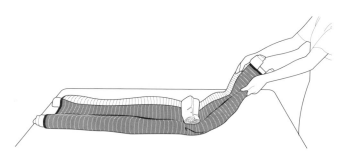

FIG. 15.6   Tissue roll for right side

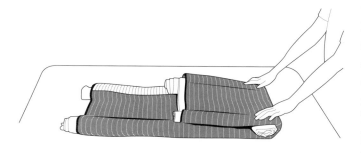

FIG. 15.7   Right side folded

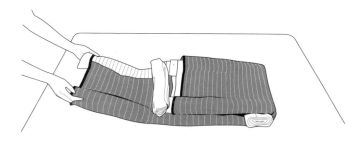

FIG. 15.8   Tissue roll for left side

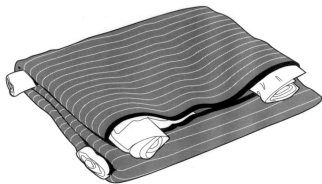

FIG. 15.9   Left side folded

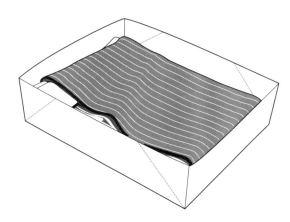

FIG. 15.10   Stored in acid-free box

If you need to store your quilts in a blanket chest or cedar chest, be very careful that the fabric does not come into direct contact with the wood, especially if the wood is unsealed like cedar. Wood gives off detrimental acids, and you will need several layers of protective material between the wood and fabric. Wrap your quilt in well-washed cotton sheeting before storing near a wood surface. If the quilt will be on a shelf, put several coats of polyurethane on the wood before placing the quilt on it. Even then, line the shelves with acid-free tissue paper.

Quilts stored in this manner need to be refolded frequently to avoid being folded on a previous crease, on a tear, or on any other wear mark. Fold a different direction each time, in halves, thirds, or in triangles like a flag.

ROLLED STORAGE

There is some controversy as to whether or not a quilt should be rolled. Some conservators say that only a single-layer textile should be rolled, while others say that quilts can benefit from this technique. If you have the space, your quilts can be rolled around a large tube that measures at least 3 inches in diameter. It should be longer than the width of the quilt. Roll the quilt loosely, with no wrinkles, and with the top to the inside if it is a pieced quilt. This puts minimum stress on the stitches. Cover the tube with cotton fabric or tissue paper. (The cover will need to be renewed once a year.) Once the quilt is rolled, cover it with a clean cotton sheet. The tubes, if strong enough, can be stored on wall brackets in a dark, clean, well-ventilated area. If the tube is too weak, run a strong rod through it (Figures 15.11 and 15.12).

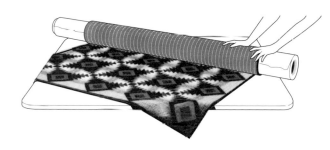

FIG. 15.11 Rolling quilt on covered tube

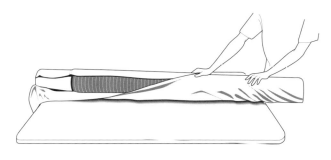

FIG. 15.12 Cover rolled quilt with muslin

All quilts need to spend some time opened out and on their backs. It is suggested by quilt curators to air them every six months or at least once a year. Lay them on the floor or on a bed for several days. On a dry, warm day, lay them on the grass to air for three or four hours. This will give you a chance to wash their coverings to remove dust and wood acids that may have been absorbed.

Once a quilt is stored, don't forget about it for long periods of time. Even with careful storage, pests can cause problems. At least once a year, the quilt needs to be refolded and have its wrapping washed or replaced. While doing this, carefully vacuum the quilt surfaces to remove moth eggs, dust particles, etc. Moth crystals in the vacuum bag will kill any insects sucked up in the cleaning process so they can't escape.

If you have problems with moths in wool or wool-filled quilts, there are several solutions. One is to dry-clean the item. You can also try freezing the quilt for about 2 months, or vacuuming then treating with moth balls (paradichlorobenzene, PDCB.) Do not use Naphthalene moth balls. One method given by Michael Kile of The Quilt Digest Press, is to use two garbage bags, one inside the other. Loosely fold the quilt and place it in the bags. Put a lot of PDCB moth balls in a cotton cloth, twist and tie at the top. Make sure this bag of moth balls sits on top of the quilt. Tightly seal the bag and leave it for at least a week, possibly two. The warmer the temperature (preferably around 70°), the better this treatment will work. Mothballs are a good general treatment for all insects.

If you feel you need to treat an area for insects, suspend a cloth bag of moth balls from the ceiling in your storage closet. The fumes are heavier than air, so the bag needs to be placed above the items you want to treat. Use a heavy concentration of PDCB for two months, rather than a small amount continuously. Do not allow the chemical to come into direct contact with the fabric.

Avoid having your best quilts around smokers. Cigarette smoke soaks into fabric faster and deeper than anything. Smoke can cause color changes and it also speeds the deterioration of the fibers in the quilt.

Because quilts are an art form and are valuable not only in dollars, but in sentimental value, they deserve special attention. A new quilt, as well as one made many years ago, can be ruined by improper storage, display, use and cleaning. Treat quilts with care, and they will bring you joy for many, many years.

HANGING AND DISPLAYING YOUR QUILTS

Quilts are generally made as functional showpieces and are of little value if stored away and not seen and enjoyed. However, care needs to be taken if the quilt is to be hung for display. Quilts on display should be rotated, so that one quilt does not hang for long periods of time. It is hard to notice changes occurring in the textiles when we see them constantly. Continued exposure is bad for the fibers and dyes of the fabrics in quilts, so do not hang a quilt for more than three months, six at the most. Store it in a dark place for awhile so that the colors can be rejuvenated and the fibers can rest for awhile.

Avoid hanging quilts where extreme temperatures and humidity are a problem. To reduce the chance of temperature variation, also avoid hanging them on an outside wall or near heating vents.

A room that is not constantly lighted is also beneficial because nothing is more harmful to textiles than light. Ultra-violet light damage is irreversible. It causes the breakdown of the dyes and pigments, accelerating the fading process. Direct sunlight is the worst, and fluorescent tube lighting is the second most damaging light source to dyes and fibers in textiles.

These light sources need to be filtered. Sunlight can be filtered by using mini-blinds, adjusting the slats down to the morning sun and up to the afternoon sun. Sheers on the windows are also a good filter. Beware of window films; the effective life of the film is five years. UV filters on florescent light tubes are recommended. The main objective is to cut out direct light rays on the fabrics. Remember, the industry standards for colorfastness to light for the cottons used in quiltmaking today is only 20 hours maximum. This makes them very vulnerable.

When choosing a place to hang a quilt, remember that the quilt is safest the further away it is from a window. If possible, put the quilt on the same wall as the window. Morning light is the most harmful to the quilt. Look around the room and see where the light is hitting throughout the day. Avoid those areas. The worst wall is opposite a window.

If the quilt will be on a bed in a sunny or bright room, it is recommended that the quilt be turned every morning. This will prevent any one area from being over-exposed to a strong light source.

If the quilt is wool, hang it for time periods shorter than three to six months to prevent drooping and stretching. Also, inspect the quilt for moths just as you would if the quilt were going to be stored.

There are safe ways and poor ways to hang a quilt for display. Never hang a quilt using nails, staples or pins. This creates severe stress in small areas and will break threads. It can also cause rust spots as well as sagging and distortion in the weave of the cloth. The weight of the quilt needs to be distributed over its entire width.

The most common way to hang today's quilts is to apply a hanging sleeve on the backside of the top width. Textile conservators offer the following tips for applying a sleeve:

1) Measure the top edge of the textile to be hung.
2) Cut a 4-inch wide strip of twill tape or cotton webbing, the desired length minus ½ inch. This should be wider than the finished width of the sleeve.
3) Make a casing (sleeve), cutting a strip of fabric 7 inches wide and the desired length plus 1 inch. Fold and sew the long edge, right sides together. Turn right side out and turn the ends in and stitch. The casing should be narrower than the twill.
4) Stitch the casing to the twill, top and bottom, leaving a slight fullness or bubble extending outward. Do not stitch the ends.
5) Hand stitch the twill on all sides to the quilt back. Go through all layers of the quilt. The top row of stitches should be spaced ½ inch apart, the bottom row spaced 1 inch apart. Be certain not to pull the stitches too tight to avoid tearing or puckering.

Another excellent way to hang a quilt is by using Velcro®. Use a 2-inch wide hook and loop tape of Velcro. Measure the top edge of the quilt to be hung. Cut a prewashed 3-inch wide strip of webbing or cotton fabric the desired length about ½ inch shorter than the actual top edge of the quilt. Machine stitch around all sides of the loop side of the 2-inch tape to fasten it to the fabric support (Figure 15.13). Position the fabric support so that it is just below the top edge of the quilt, about ½ inch. It is important to keep the strip in a straight line, although the top edge of the quilt may not be straight.

Hand sew the fabric support to the quilt at all sides. Stitch through all layers of the quilt. The top

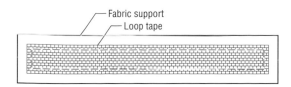

FIG. 15.13 Stitch loop side to fabric support

row of stitches should be spaced ½ inch apart. The lower row may be spaced 1 inch apart. Use straight running stitches. Be careful not to pull the thread too tightly, as it may tear the fabric or cause puckering. Use only 100% cotton thread (Figure 15.14).

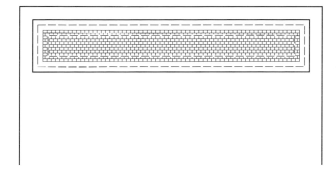

FIG. 15.14 Stitch fabric support to quilt

To mount the quilt on the wall, use a 1 by 3-inch board that corresponds to the size of the top edge of the quilt. Seal it with polyurethane to prevent acid migration and discoloration of the quilt. Staple the hook side of the tape to the board (Figure 15.15). Attach the board to the wall. Press the top edge of the quilt to the loop side mounted on the board. Make adjustments if the quilt does not hang properly (Figure 15.16).

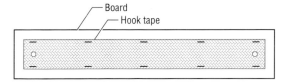

FIG. 15.15 Staple hook side to mounting board

If the quilt is fragile or heavy, it will need extra support. This is especially true of old crazy quilts. Use a well-washed backing fabric and baste the quilt onto it. Run horizontal rows of hand basting stitches across the quilt and through the backing fabric about every 12 inches from the top to the bottom. Try to make the stitches invisible by following the

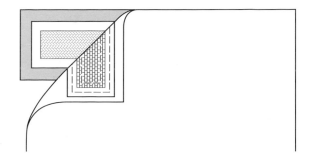

FIG. 15.16 Attaching quilt to mounting board

pattern of the quilt top. Do not pull stitches tight. Apply the sleeve to the quilt as discussed above. The backing fabric, not the quilt, takes the strain of hanging.

For maximum support, a backing fabric can be stretched over a wooden frame. The wood should be given a polyurethane finish to seal in the wood acids. Staple the backing fabric to the backside of the frame. Then baste the quilt to the backing fabric as shown above. The use of a curved needle is helpful.

There are several different types of rods for hanging quilts. If using any wood product such as a closet rod, dowel or 1-by-3-inch board, make sure that the wood has been sealed with polyurethane. You can also use a plexiglass rod or a decorative curtain rod.

We often have sections of quilts or pieced squares that we wish to frame and display under glass. To prepare the pieces, baste the piece to a cotton fabric on a wooden stretcher that fits inside the picture frame.

A spacer or mat is needed to prevent the glass from touching the fabric. Mold and mildew can grow where the fabric and glass touch, making this very important. If glass is used on the front, allow for air circulation from the back. Instead of the paper usually applied to the back of the frame, staple a cotton dust cover to the back instead.

With proper care, your quilts can be on display and enjoyed for years. They deserve the same special consideration that any other piece of artwork would.

Conclusion

TODAY'S QUILTERS ARE FINDING IT MORE AND MORE difficult to find the time to produce the many quilts in their heads. We have developed and mastered machine piecing to compensate, but instead of gaining more quilts, we get more quilt tops and then guilt for not finishing them.

Heirloom Machine Quilting is meant to be a means to an end. It is my sincere hope that this book will be the key to getting those tops finished and on the beds. If we continue to explore new and faster methods, we will keep quilting alive and well. Let the pictures inspire you to create your own heirloom quality quilts in feasible amounts of time. Work through the exercises, and enjoy!

Quilting Designs

T HE PATTERNS IN THIS SECTION are all "continuous line" patterns. Refer to page 17 for how to make your own stencils from these patterns.

Follow the dash lines for quilting. The arrows are for your reference only, and do not need to be marked onto the quilt.

When starting, begin at the star, and work in numerical order. Border designs such as those on pages 118 and 119 can be two ways. You can start each line from the same end or stitch from one end to the other, then reverse direction and come back on the second line without breaking your thread.

Feel free to enlarge or reduce these designs to any size needed for your personal use.

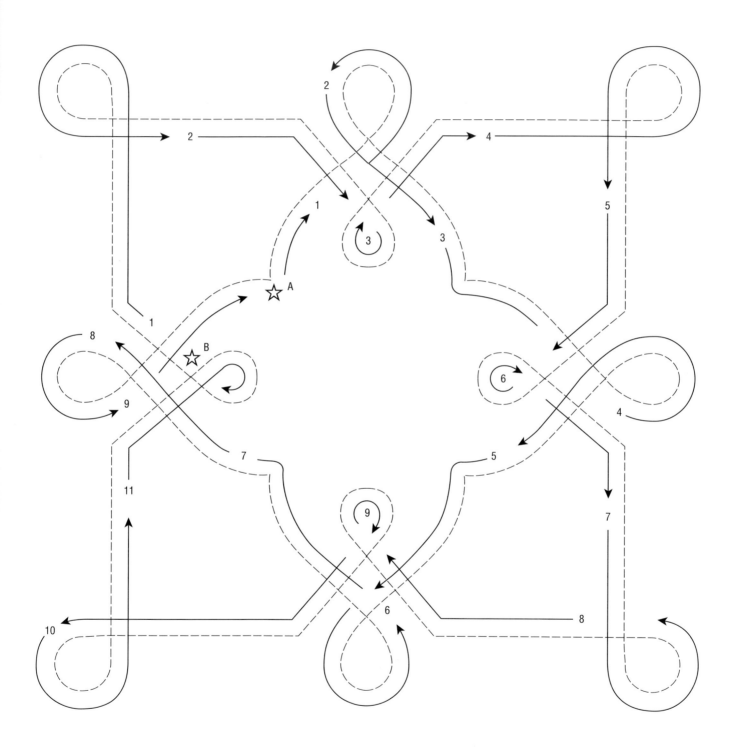

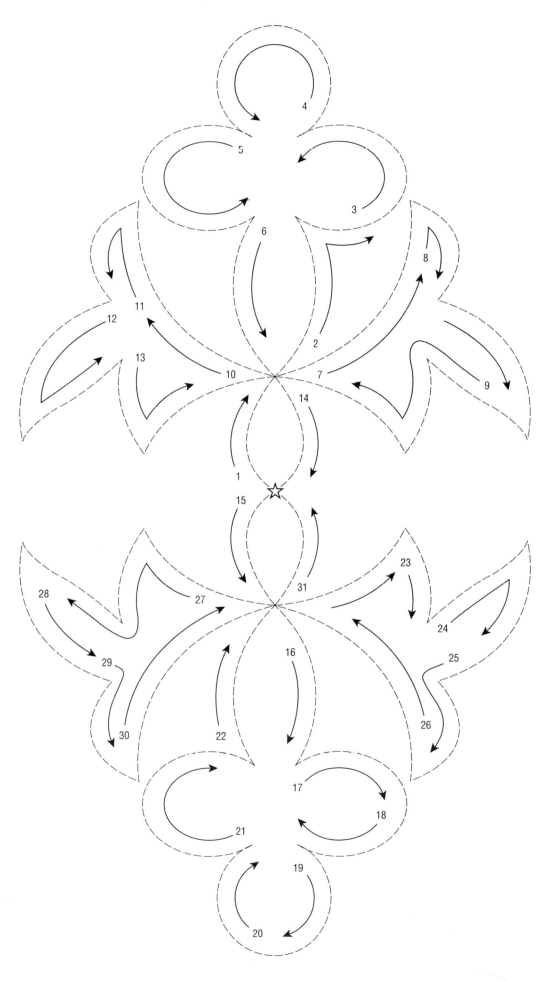

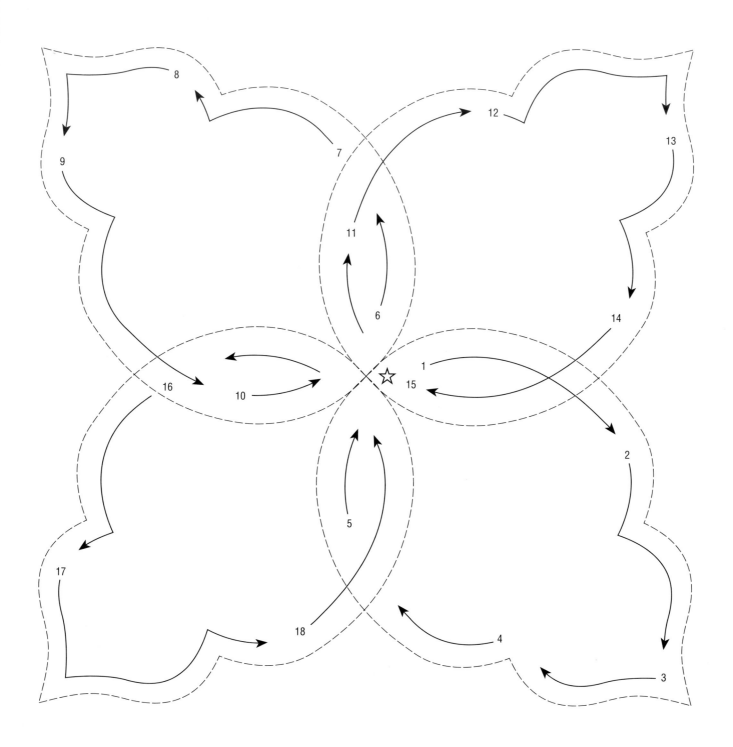

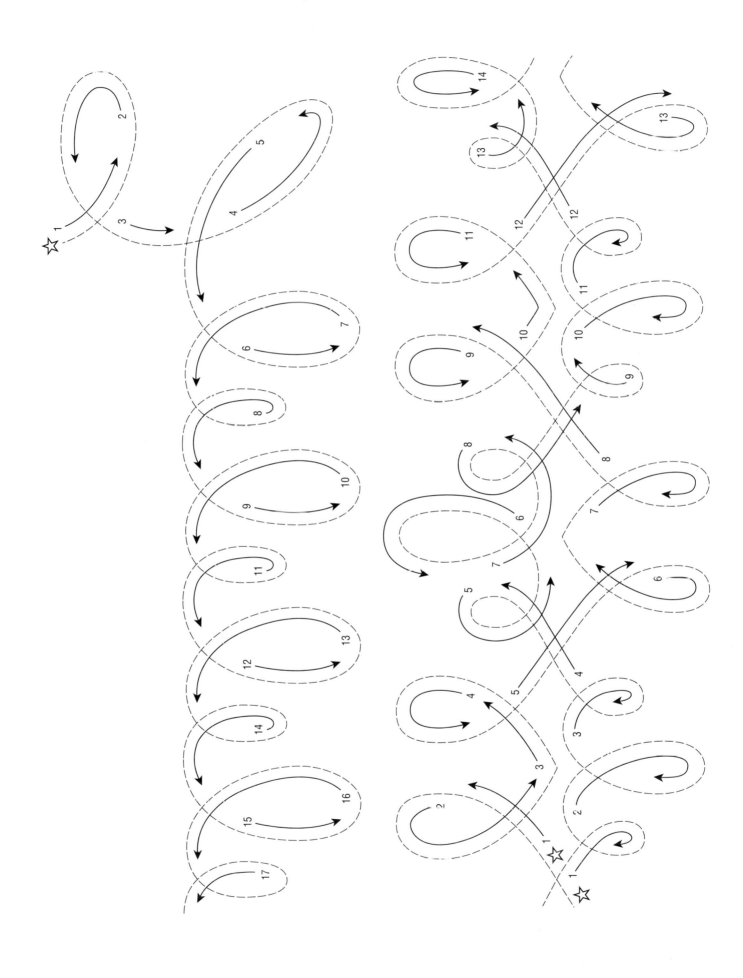

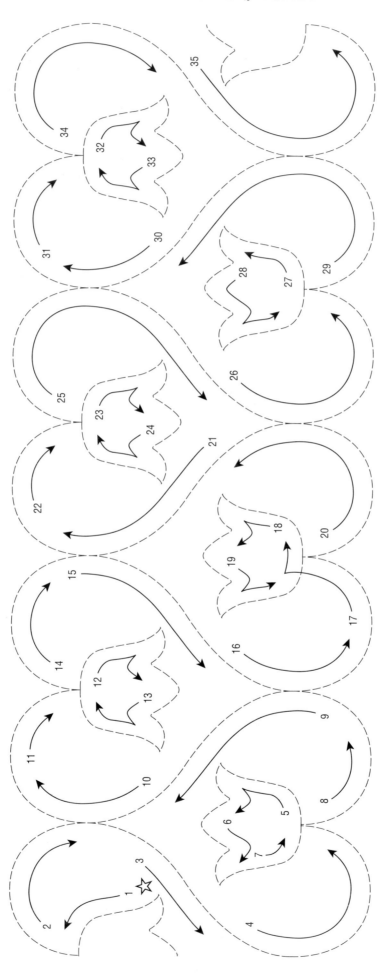

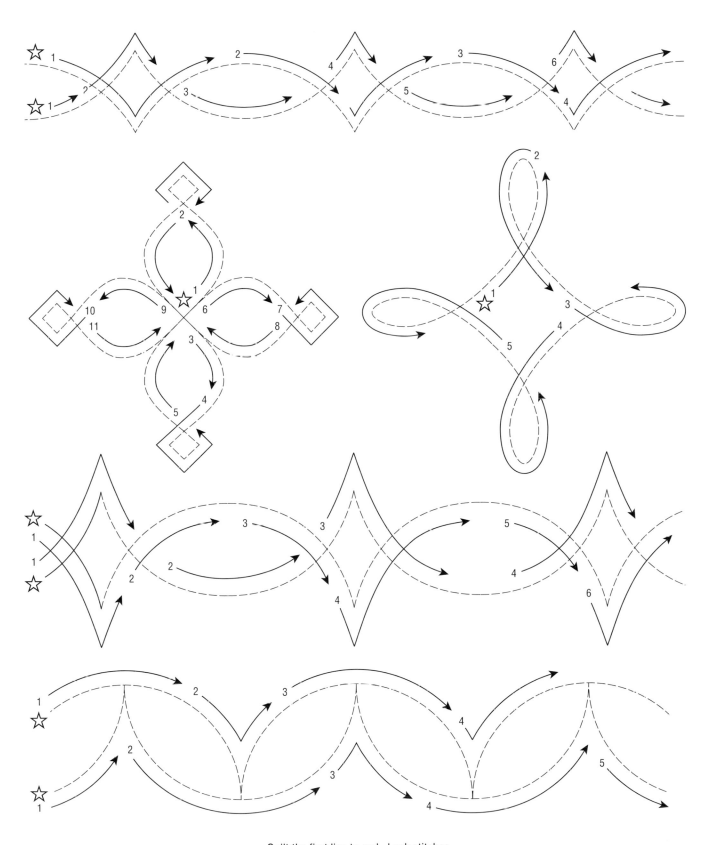

Quilt the first line to end. Lock stitches.
Return to second line and quilt to end.

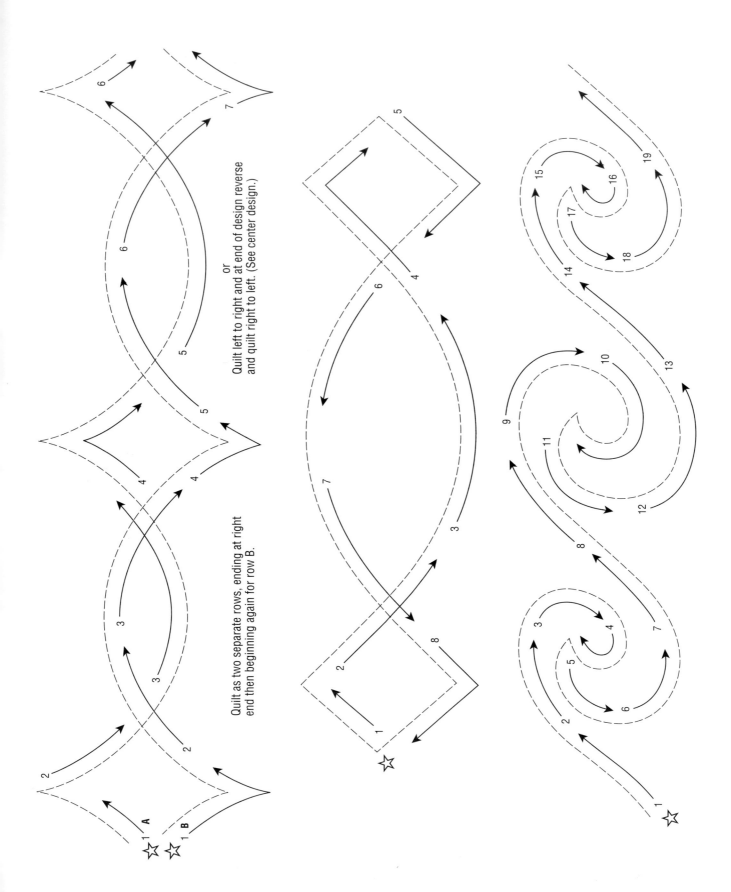

or
Quilt left to right and at end of design reverse
and quilt right to left. (See center design.)

Quilt as two separate rows, ending at right
end then beginning again for row B.

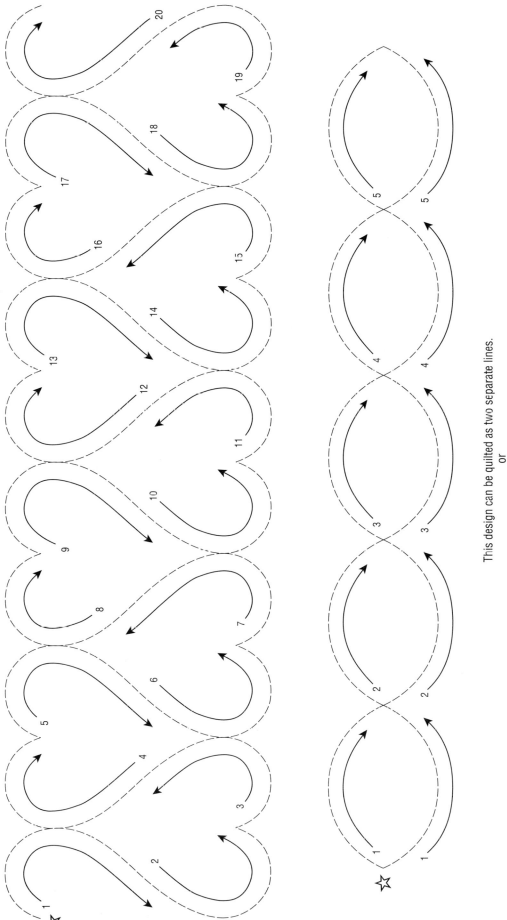

This design can be quilted as two separate lines.
or
Quilt left to right, then quilt right to left back
to the beginning.

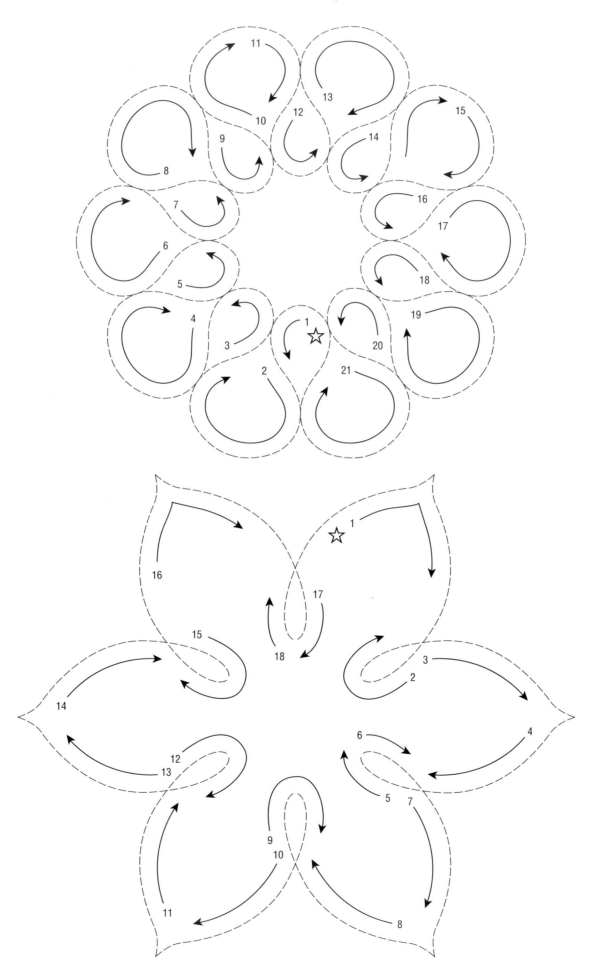

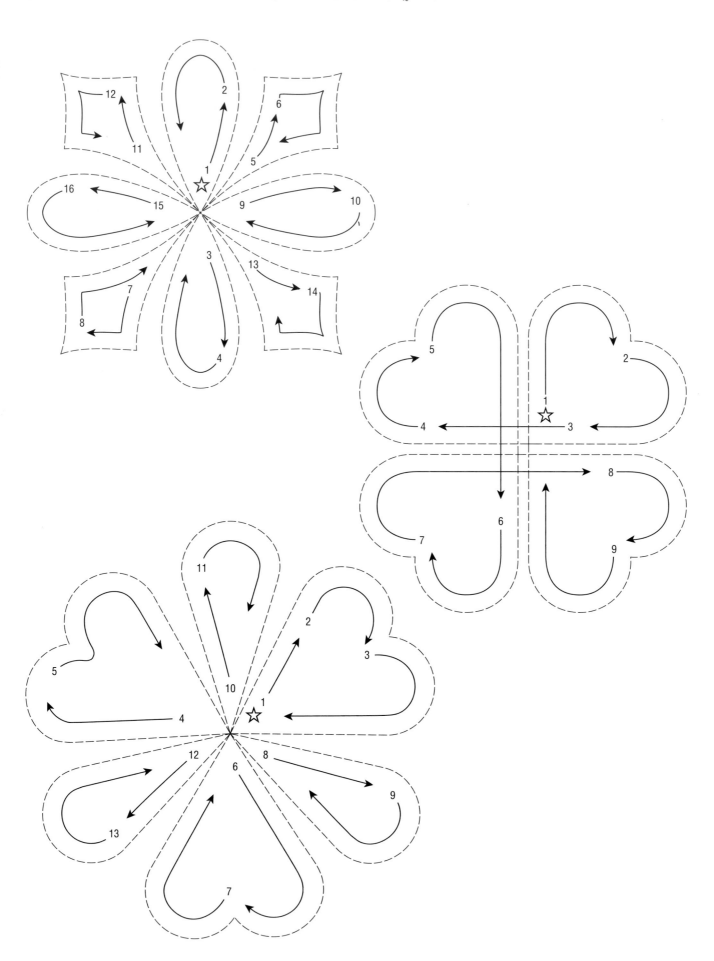

Wholesale Suppliers

WHOLESALE SUPPLIERS for products mentioned in this book:

American Quilter (stencil burner/hot pen)
P.O. Box 7455
Menlo Park, CA 94025

Bernina of America (sewing cabinet and machine)
534 W. Chestnut
Hinsdale, IL 60521

C&T Publishing (fine quilting books)
P.O. Box 1456
Lafayette, CA 94549

Edge Distributing (Easy Wash)
P.O. Box 307
Park Ridge, IL 60068

Fairfield Processing Corporation
P.O. Box 1130
Danbury, CT 06813

Inglis Publications Products (DBK plastic)
P.O. Box 266
Dexter, MI 48130

Swiss-Metrosene, Inc. (cotton sewing thread)
1107 Marlin Dr.
Roseville, CA 95661

Powell Publications (quilting pattern books)
Box 513
Edmonds, WA 98020

Sew-Art International (invisible thread, Tear-Away)
P.O. Box 550
Bountiful, UT 84010

Taos Mountain Wool Works
P.O. Box 327
Arroyo Hondo, NM 87513

The Stearns Technical Textile Co.
   (batting and Ensure)
Mountain Mist Division
100 Williams Street
Cincinnati, OH 45215-6316

Uni Unique Products (extension table)
3200 Dutton #225
Santa Rosa, CA 95404

Consumers can mail order all products mentioned in this book directly from Harriet at:

Harriet's Treadle Arts
6390 West 44th Ave.
Wheatridge, CO 80033
(303) 424-2742

Bibliography

Beyer, Jinny. *The Art and Technique of Creating Medallion Quilts.* McLean, Va.: EPM Publications, Inc., 1982.

Cory, Pepper. *Quilting Designs From The Amish.* Lafayette, Ca.: C & T Publishing, 1985.

Donahue, Nancy. *Quilting-As-You-Go Guide.* Chino, Ca.: The Ink Spot, 1979.

Emery, Linda Goodmon. *A Treasury of Quilting Designs.* Paducah, Ky.: The American Quilter's Society, 1990.

Fanning, Robbie and Tony. *The Complete Book Of Machine Quilting.* Radnor, Pa.: Chilton Book Co., 1980.

Johannah, Barbara. *Continuous Curve Quilting the Machine Pieced Quilt.* Menlo Park, Ca.: Pride of the Forest, 1980.

Joseph, Marjory L. *Introductory Textile Science.* New York: Holt, Rienhart and Winston, 1986.

Macho, Linda. *Quilting Patterns.* New York: Dover Publications, 1984.

Orlofsky, Patsy. *The Quilt Digest 2.* San Francisco: The Quilt Digest Press, 1984

Thompson, Shirley. *The Finishing Touch.* Edmonds, Wa.: Powell Publications, 1980.

_____ . *It's Not a Quilt Until It's Quilted.* Edmonds, Wa.: Powell Publications, 1980.

_____ . *Old-Time Quilting Designs.* Edmonds, Wa.: Powell Publications, 1989.

Wyatt, Nancy Conlin. *"Textile Conservation Consultant."* Paris, Tx. Photocopy.

Zadel, Lauri Linch. *"Wool Batts: From Sheep to Quilt."* Quilters Newsletter Magazine, May 1986, page 34.

Index

About the Author

HARRIET HARGRAVE, quilt shop owner and teacher, has been teaching machine arts and quilting since 1976. She has been teaching throughout the United States since 1985, as well as in England, Ireland, Canada, Hawaii, and Australia.

Harriet comes from a long line of quilters. Her grandmother, aunts, and mother were all avid quilters. Her mother continues to quilt, as well as help run and operate their quilt store. Hand quilting and appliqué never appealed to Harriet, but quilts always lured her. She has continually looked for ways to adapt sewing machine techniques to quilts, being very careful to keep them looking hand-made.

Harriet has a degree in Textiles and Clothing from Colorado State University. She owns and operates Harriet's Treadle Arts in Wheat Ridge, Colorado, and lives in Arvada, Colorado, with her daughter Carrie.

Oᴛʜᴇʀ ꜰɪɴᴇ ꜰQᴜɪʟᴛɪɴɢ ʙᴏᴏᴋs available from C & T Publishing:

A Celebration of Hearts, Jean Wells and Marina Anderson

An Amish Adventure, Roberta Horton

Baltimore Album Quilts, Historic Notes and Antique Patterns, Elly Sienkiewicz

Baltimore Beauties and Beyond, Elly Sienkiewicz

Boston Commons Quilt, Blanche Young and Helen Young Frost

Calico and Beyond, Roberta Horton

Contemporary Sampler, Katie Pasquini

Crazy Quilt Handbook, Judith Montano

Crosspatch, Pepper Cory

Diamond Patchwork, Jeffrey Gutcheon

Fans, Jean Wells

Fine Feathers, Marianne Fons

Flying Geese Quilt, Blanche Young and Helen Young Frost

Friendship's Offering, Susan McKelvey

Irish Chain Quilt, Blanche Young and Helen Young Frost

Landscapes and Illusions, Joen Wolfrom

Let's Make Waves, Marianne Fons and Liz Porter

Light and Shadows, Susan McKelvey

Mandala, Katie Pasquini

Mariner's Compass, Judy Mathieson

New Lone Star Handbook, Blanche Young and Helen Young Frost

Perfect Pineapples, Jane Hall and Dixie Haywood

Picture This, Jean Wells and Marina Anderson

Plaids and Stripes, Roberta Horton

Quilting Designs From the Amish, Pepper Cory

Quilting Designs From Antique Quilts, Pepper Cory

Radiant Nine Patch, Blanche Young

Stained Glass Quilting Technique, Roberta Horton

Trip Around the World Quilts, Blanche Young and Helen Young Frost

Visions: Quilts of a New Decade, Quilt San Diego

Working in Miniature, Becky Schaefer

Wearable Art For Real People, Mary Mashuta

3 Dimensional Design, Katie Pasquini

For more information write for a free catalog from:
C & T Publishing
P.O. Box 1456
Lafayette, CA 94553